# Filipino Spirit World

## A Challenge to the Church

Rodney L. Henry

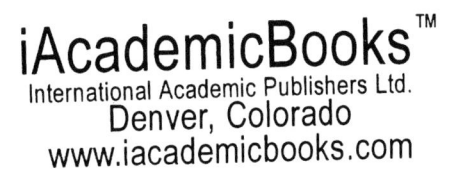

**iAcademicBooks**™
International Academic Publishers Ltd.
Denver, Colorado
www.iacademicbooks.com

All rights reserved. No part of this publication may be reproduced, stored in a retrieval system or transmitted in any form or by any means without the written permission of the publishers.

iAcademicBooks, an imprint of
International Academic Publishers Ltd.
P. O. Box 26290
Colorado Springs, Colorado 80918
USA

*Unless otherwise noted, all Scripture quotations are taken from*
New American Standard Bible, *copyright © 1960, 1962, 1963, 1968, 1971, 1972, 1973 by the Lockman Foundation. Used by permission.*

Filipino Spirit World
*Copyright © 1986 OMF Literature Inc.*

Library of Congress Cataloging-in-Publication Data

Henry, Rodney L.
  Filipino spirit world : a challenge to the church / Rodney L. Henry.
    p. cm.
  Includes bibliographical references and index.
  ISBN 1-58868-084-3 (pbk.)
  1. Christianity and culture--Philippines. 2. Animism--Philippines. 3. Philippines--Religious life and customs. I. Title.

BR1260 .H46 2001
261.5'13'09599--dc21

2001016647

# Contents

| | | |
|---|---|---|
| Foreword | | 4 |
| Introduction | | 8 |
| 1 | Folk Christianity | 12 |
| 2 | Western and Filipino Worldviews | 26 |
| 3 | Theological Foundations: The God Among Spirits | 49 |
| 4 | The Angelic Spirit World | 56 |
| 5 | From Lucifer To Satan | 74 |
| 6 | The Demonic Spirit World | 86 |
| 7 | Demonization | 97 |
| 8 | Discerning Supernatural Powers | 117 |
| 9 | The Test of Trust | 134 |
| 10 | Filipinizing the Church | 149 |
| 11 | Teaching and Alternatives: Keys to Victory for the Church | 158 |
| Bibliography | | 172 |
| Index | | 187 |
| About the Author | | 194 |

# Foreword

As the jet liner lifted from the runway, a Christian man was buckled into the center seat of the three on his side of the aisle. He looked to his right and left, and noticed that the two men seated beside him were well dressed, but obviously of very different backgrounds.

Clouds momentarily swept past the window as he introduced himself to the gentleman in the window seat. Customary exchanges revealed he was an aeronautical engineer, bound for a technical convention in a foreign city. As they talked, the engineer mentioned he had personally been part of the design team that developed the aircraft on which they were riding. With bright sunlight sparkling off aluminum visible outside the window, the engineer began to explain the structure of the wing, the function of each cover plate, and the stress factors which necessitated the many rivets. When the Christian turned the conversation to spiritual matters, he soon learned the engineer was an atheist; there was no need for God in his mechanistic world.

About the time the stewardesses served dinner, the Christian introduced himself to the gentleman near the aisle. He was amazed and delighted to learn the man was an honoree, selected by his developing nation as a model farmer. This

## FOREWORD

flight would take him home, after visiting farms and observing farming methods in a dozen or more developed and developing nations. Further conversation revealed that the model farmer had little education, and had never flown in an airplane before he began this trip. Again the Christian turned the conversation to things spiritual, but this time discovered his seatmate was an animist. The world in which he lived was populated and controlled by spirits.

Twenty years have passed since I first heard Dr. Francis Schaeffer paint this imaginary picture. Dr. Schaeffer asked, "Which of the two seatmates holds a worldview closer to the Christian's?" Although many Christians would like to be identified with the highly educated, highly influential, highly technological world of the aeronautical engineer, the truth is that his view is very different from the universe presented in the Bible. It is the animistic farmer who knows, like the Christian, that the world consists of two halves — one seen and the other one unseen — and that *both halves are equally real.*

Unfortunately, the church has not always acknowledged this fact. Beginning during the eighteenth century "Enlightenment" in Europe, Western philosophy and science discovered that most human observations could be described and predicted with mathematical models. Scientists became more and more confident that the universe was a strictly natural phenomenon, and that the natural world was the only world that exists. If we cannot see it, feel it, measure it, or weigh it, it does not exist.

Confronted by successive triumphs in the fields of science and technology based on these ideas, most church leaders and theologians sought a strategic retreat. They suggested that religious "truths" do not really relate to this world. We encounter God only in "spiritual" experiences, but He does not work in this world or directly affect our lives in any way. Simple people believe God, angels, the devil, heaven, hell, and miracles, exist, but many theologians concluded this was only "spiritually" true. They began to teach that these things do not exist in the same way the natural world exists, and most important of all, there is no interaction between the natural and the spiritual realms.

For most of this century, the church (both Roman Catholic and Protestant — including Evangelicals) has promoted (by example, if not precept) this worldview, based on the naturalistic assumptions of Western culture. Perhaps no other heresy has more effectively penetrated the church or blunted its work in the world.

Filipinos have never been deceived. They know the spirit world is real and that it directly affects events in our daily lives. In fifteen years of teaching Bible college and seminary students in this country, I have yet to discuss this topic with a student who has not personally encountered the spirit world experiences of an immediate family member. When Roman Catholic and Protestant missionaries attempt to explain away spirit phenomena, they only destroy their own credibility. A Westernized church can meet some, but not all, of the spiritual needs of Filipinos.

This book shows us how to change that pattern. It shows us how a Biblical theology of the spirit world can account for phenomena frequently encountered in Philippine society. It shows how the Church can be more culturally relevant by becoming more biblical.

Rodney Henry is an evangelical Protestant, but this book will be welcomed by all who desire the Church in this country to respond more authentically to Philippine culture and to the Bible as the Word of God.

I have known Rodney Henry and his wife, Camille, since January 1980, shortly after their arrival in this country. Over

## FOREWORD

the past five years, I have rarely visited Cebu City without sampling their hospitality. I am pleased to commend this book as a significant contribution to the Filipino Church. Western missionaries (new and old), theological students and all who seek an authentic and Biblical Christianity will share my indebtedness to the Henrys.

Robert W. Ferris

# Introduction

When we speak of animism, many of us immediately think of "primitive people." The word "animism" carries with it for many hearers a concept of ignorance and superstition which could be confronted and easily destroyed by education and Christianity.

This is simply not the case. In this book we will see that animism is not ignorant and superstitious, but a different way in which people explain the world around them. Its strength lies in its emphasis on the everyday concerns of people.

Cross-cultural Christian workers (i.e., missionaries) often go to countries where the people are said to believe in one of the "great religions" (Hinduism, Islam, Christianity, Buddhism, etc.). Before going to that country a study of the religion of the target group is made. Once on the field, the worker is usually surprised to discover that the majority of the people have little or no knowledge of the "great religion" which they claimed to believe.

The majority of Filipinos are Catholics. However, a superficial look at Filipino Christianity may cause one to draw the conclusion that Filipinos are not very "religious." This conclusion can be drawn by examining what Filipinos do and believe in relation to their "great religion." However, if the

*INTRODUCTION*

cross-cultural worker will look further into the everyday lives of the people, he will probably discover that the people are very "religious" in certain matters regarding their belief in the spirit world around them. This is, of course, the result of their animistic worldview.

During my first term as a missionary in Cebu City, after I had been in the country for four months, an event took place that made me wonder. I was asked to preach at a funeral service for the mother of a young Christian man. The mother who died was a Roman Catholic, the father was a local witch doctor, and the son was a new Christian.

The witch doctor was in charge of the wake and it had some very animistic elements. For example, they were all very careful to make sure that no tears fell on the coffin. At that time I was very confused by all that was going on. I did not have then the skills for observation and analysis I have now. From the animistic wake in the home, the entire procession moved to the Roman Catholic Church. Here the family was very busy trying to gather enough money to pay the priest so that they would be able to have a mass said on behalf of the dead woman.

After the mass, everyone moved to the grave site to have a Protestant preaching service with singing. When the preaching was over, I was led out of the cemetery, and some leaves were taken out of the witch doctor's pocket and put on the small fire. Then each person "bathed" himself in the smoke of the fire as he left to go home.

This event left me very confused. My confusion was over the fact that these people saw no conflict between their Christian belief, and their animistic beliefs and practices. That day, and for many days after, I asked many questions about what had taken place. Each time, I was answered with a nervous laugh and the response, "we Filipinos are a superstitious people." There were open lines of communication in every area, except that of animistic beliefs.

When I confronted the other evangelical missionaries on this subject, I got the same basic answer that I had gotten from the Filipinos, that, "they are a superstitious people." When I asked about the animistic beliefs and practices of their church members, they didn't seem to think that it was a problem in their group.

Midway through my first term, I took a course on animism under Dr. Paul Hiebert through the In-Service Program offered by the Fuller Theological Seminary, School of World Mission. This course gave me tools which I needed to explore this phenomenon in the Philippines. By taking the course while I was on the field, there was constant interaction between the course work and the context of the Philippines. Following my first term of service, I returned to Fuller Seminary to continue research and to do a Master of Theology in Missiology (Th.M.) thesis on this area.

Several anonymous interviews are included in this book. The interviewees' names must remain unknown because many of those interviewed fear that others would label them as ignorant or superstitious. They are highly educated and successful people. They were open with me because I was not judgmental. Others who were interviewed about the spirit world are evangelical pastors. They fear that they would be judged as heretical or even demonic. So in the interest of those interviewed, I will not identify any of them.

My missionary service was spent in the Visayas. Consequently, the worldview, practices and terminology will reflect this region more than others.

There are many who should be thanked in these pages for their contribution to this work, but I will specifically mention only two. I must recognize the work of Dr. Paul Hiebert, my mentor at Fuller Theological Seminary, where I received my

*INTRODUCTION*

Master of Theology in Missiology. Over half of this book is from my thesis. I also wish to thank Paul Healy, the director of Corpus Christi Foundation, for hours spent editing the text. His help in articulating ideas and arranging materials was invaluable. The contribution and help of these two fine men can be found on every page but the errors I must claim for myself.

# 1
# FOLK CHRISTIANITY

The universe is a wonderful and complicated place. Science has tried to bring the universe into man's intellectual reach. Yet, even for modern educated man, most mysteries of the universe are unexplained. How much more mysterious is this universe to people who have not been confronted with the wonders of science. For both the scientist and the common man, the universe is full of unexplainable, unpredictable, and unexpected mysteries.

Religions all over the world serve the very important function of trying to explain to man these mysteries of the universe. Religious beliefs help people to organize this mysterious universe by defining man's relationship with nature (or god), and also his relationship with his fellow man. Explanations about what has gone on before man, and what will happen to man at death help to reduce his fears about the unknown. Religions are systems of explanation (Hiebert 1976:372).

Christians believe that God is the Creator of this universe and is still in control of it. This is not revealed to man by way of his intelligence. Christians believe certain things about the nature of the universe, the nature of God, the nature of man, and the ultimate destiny of man, and they then organize their universe and their lives based on the central concept of a Creator God who reveals Himself to man.

Animism is another system of explanation. It is based on a central belief in spirits whose power can be manipulated through formulas, rituals, or words (Nida 1975:5). Animistic religions do not have creeds or bodies of literature from which we can extract their beliefs. Yet there is a set of assumptions and beliefs by which they live and organize the universe. It was an animistic religion which was in existence in the Philippines when Ferdinand Magellan arrived in 1521 with Roman Catholicism (Rich 1970:198).

## Pre-Spanish Religion of the Filipino

Filipino history before the arrival of the Spaniards reveals a society with its roots in the family. The family was the center for education and religion. Even before the Spaniards came, the inhabitants of these islands were teaching their children to read and write using a Malayan alphabet. They had music, and there is evidence of fine art. The rice terraces of Banaue show the sophistication of the engineering skills of the early Filipino. These early inhabitants were certainly not primitive people waiting to be "civilized" by a European culture (Gowing 1967:20).

As was previously mentioned, the pre-Spanish people of these islands were religiously animistic, in that their religion was centered on the spirit world. Though they believed there were many classes and types of spirits, they had a high or supreme god concept, and a belief in an afterlife with their departed ancestors (Rich 1970:199).

## A remote, supreme god

Their supreme god was called by various names (*Bathala*, *Laon*, or *Kabunian*) depending on the region, but he was a god who was aloof and very distant from man (Skivington 1970:41).

This god was too "far away" or "different" to be approached by man. He was in charge of the universe and in control of man's fate, so that a person's fortune or misfortune was said to be the result of this god's will.

The will of the supreme god and the customs and mores of the early Filipino were one and the same. To violate the customs and mores of the group was the same as offending the will of the supreme god, which would result in *gaba* (a curse).

## Less remote lower gods

More accessible to the pre-Spanish Filipino were the lower gods called *anito*. These spirit beings were in charge of the affairs of everyday life. They controlled such things as birth, death, sickness, war, weather, agriculture, spiritual relationships, human relationships, protection of the family and village, fishing, hunting and giving information for making difficult decisions (divination). These spirit beings filled nature by living in trees, caves, and rivers. People felt that these beings would harm them if they got the chance (Rich 1970:199).

> The Filipinos believed in a myriad of environmental spirits which actively participated in their life ways. Idols were carved in representation of these spirits (Jocano 1975:40).

Life was very ordered in this belief system, and the violation of this order (taboo) could bring the wrath of these spirits on the violator, his family, and his village. The only way that these spirit beings could be appeased was through sacrifices. These sacrifices would come in various forms depending on the lower god who was to be appeased. The sacrifice could be rice, fruit, *lana* (coconut oil), or *tuba* (coconut wine) given in the context of ritual and worship. The idea was to bring back the favor of the offended lower god so that *panalangin* (grace) would be restored (Phelan 1959:23).

> Animals and fowls commonly used as sacrificial "objects" are goats, chickens, pigs and carabaos. Most of the sacrifices were given for the following reasons: (1) recovery of a sick person; (2) prosperous voyage of those embarking on the sea; (3) a good harvest in the sowed lands; (4) a propitious result in wars; (5) successful delivery in childbirth; and (6) a happy outcome in married life (Jocano 1975:41).

This ritual sacrifice to appease the *anito* was a vital part of the religious life of the pre-Spanish Filipino. Though anyone was allowed to perform the sacrifice, the family would usually call on the services of a religious practitioner. The religious practitioners were usually women and variously called *babaylan, baylanes* or *catalonan* (Rich 1970:200). Their services were secured to perform these sacrifices because the ritual needed to be performed precisely in order to achieve the desired results (Kroeber 1928:187).

> These ceremonies were performed by religious specialists. Most important among these specialists were the *catalonans* among Tagalogs and the *baylanes* among the Bisayans. These people were responsible for solving the religious and medical problems of the people (Jocano 1975:41).

## Ancestral spirits

Ancestral spirits were another class of spirit beings to be worshipped and appeased. The ancestral spirits in one's own family were for the good of family members still living, provided that those living paid proper respect to these spirits.

This required paying homage, giving sacrifices, and praying to these dead ancestors so that they would respond favorably to the needs of living family members. Ancestral spirits were able to intercede with the supreme god on behalf of the living, thus making it very important to maintain a proper relationship with these spirit beings. The ancestral spirits of an enemy village or family would be seen as evil and very hostile to their living enemies. (Rich 1970:199).

## Lesser spirit beings and objects with spiritual power

There were countless other kinds of spirit world beings which inhabited the universe of the pre-Spanish Filipino. These ranged from beings which had purely spiritual qualities to humans who had spiritual powers. For example, the *wakwak* was a witch who could detach the top part of her body from the waist. The top portion of her body could fly around at night looking for victims to satisfy her appetite for human flesh. The *aswang* was a witch who could turn into an animal and prey on victims at night. In general, these spirit beings were greatly feared.

Protection against these malevolent spirits was provided through the possession of amulets called *anting-anting*. These magical objects possessed power against the spirit world and gave this power to the person possessing them. These amulets helped to relieve some of the fear of spirit beings for these early Filipinos.

The religious life of the pre-Spanish Filipino was based on a fear of angering the spirit world by violating a taboo. These spirits were seen as hostile and waiting for any reason to inflict their wrath on people. The wrath of the spirit world could come on a person because a spirit was hit by an object inadvertently thrown out of a window at night, or by a woman hitting a spirit with a *palo-palo,* the paddle used for washing clothes. It was man's task to live in harmony with the spirit world and by so doing, avoid *gaba* and receive *panalangin.*

For pre-Spanish Filipinos, spirit beings both inhabited nature and were one with nature. The spirits in control of the universe were what westerners would call "nature." So, controlling the spirits in nature was the same as controlling nature. Though they lived in fear of the spirit world, they also attempted to control it through the use of rituals, amulets, idols and other magical objects.

## Life after death

These people had a belief in an afterlife. This life to come was supposed to be of the same sort as the present life, with the dead being taken to *kaluwalhatian* (glory). The position of people in the afterlife was not based on the morality of a person's actions while living. It was based on the same socio-economic situation which a person occupied while alive on earth. So poverty and slavery were the worst situations on earth because that would be the person's lot in the afterlife (Gutierrez 1976:252).

## ADDING ROMAN CATHOLICISM

In 1521, Ferdinand Magellan arrived in Cebu and claimed the islands for Spain. One week later, he baptized the king, queen, and the entire population of Cebu (Latourette 1975:935).

As was the case in other parts of the world colonized and evangelized by the Spaniards, the Roman Catholic Church believed that Filipino traditions and folkways could be kept, as long as they did not conflict with the teachings of the Catholic Church (Toliver 1970:212). The Spanish clergy had three basic requirements for the baptism of adults: a person must have a monogamous marriage, repent from the sins of his past life, and believe in the efficacy of the sacrament of baptism (salvation by baptism).

To this were added some of the other basic elements of the Roman Catholic institution: the *Ave Maria*, the Ten Commandments, and the Lord's Prayer (Rich 1970:201). Very early, the Spanish clergy began baptizing children and teaching the rituals and doctrines of the Catholic Church. This teaching was centered on the church. This was an attempt to shift the center for religious education from the home to the church. The result was that the church was the center for teaching the old religion of animism.

## Two different emphases

Though Filipino animism had a mythology that explained the creation of the world, man's beginnings, god's nature and man's ultimate destiny, these "higher" or "ultimate" concerns were not the backbone of their animism. Filipino animism was more concerned with the practical areas of everyday life. The pre-Spanish animist was much more concerned with agriculture and hunting than with his origin and ultimate destiny. Animism was weakest in these areas of higher or ultimate concerns, while it was very strong in areas of everyday living.

With the coming of the Spaniards, the Filipino animist was confronted with a religion which was and is very strong on these higher or ultimate concerns. Roman Catholicism taught a different story than the one from their own traditions, but one which was not completely incompatible with their own understanding of their supreme god: God was the Creator of the universe; man had sinned and needed salvation; Jesus came to earth to be the sacrifice for man's sin; and now, God had given the authority of salvation to the Roman Catholic Church. The Filipino only needed to repent of his past sins, and be baptized by the priest in order to have his ultimate concerns (salvation) taken care of.

## "Folk Catholicism"

By 1590 about half of the country had been baptized. Yet, from then until now, the Roman Catholic clergy has realized that the religion that was produced was not really Roman Catholic, but an interesting blend of Roman Catholicism and animism that is often called "folk Catholicism" (Latourette 1975:936). A good deal has been written on folk Catholicism, both pro and con.

Father Vitaliano R. Gorospe, S.J., in the article entitled, "Christian Renewal of Filipino Values," states,

> Consequently, even today, especially in the rural areas, we find merely the external trappings of Catholic belief and practice superimposed on the original pattern of pre-Christian superstitions and rituals (1966:37).

Another perspective on folk Catholicism is that of Father Jaime Bulatao, S.J. In the article "Split-level Christianity," he contends that Filipinos possess two inconsistent religious systems. The Catholicism which Filipinos profess is not the same as the life that they lead. Bulatao describes "split-level Christianity" as the "coexistence within the same person of two or more thought-and-behavior systems which are inconsistent with each other" (1966:2).

## Coexistence of two religions

There is another option for describing this interesting blend of Roman Catholicism and animism called folk Catholicism. Folk Catholicism is not merely the external appearances of two inconsistent religions existing in the same person as the Roman Catholics priests have suggested above. Folk Catholicism is the coexistence of two religions in the same person without inconsistencies. The Roman Catholic aspect of folk

Catholicism deals with the higher or ultimate concerns, while the animistic aspect deals with the concerns of everyday living. These are two separate thought and behavior systems, each dealing with different areas of life.

Roman Catholicism had little or nothing to say about the everyday concerns of the Filipino. There was no theology of weather, fishing, hunting, where to build a house or how to cure spirit-caused sicknesses. The Filipino assumed that this was the domain of his own spirit religion. The Spanish clergy and nobility passed judgment on the everyday animistic religion of the Filipino as being superstitious and sometimes even demonic. But because the church gave no substitute for these practical, everyday concerns of the common *tao* (people), the belief in the power of the spirit world continues until today as the everyday religion of the Filipino. Leonardo Mercado, in his book, *Filipino Religious Psychology*, says, "Apparently the Filipino is still an animist at heart, in spite of four centuries of Roman Catholicism" (1979:XIV).

Chr. Vandenbogaert, a Roman Catholic, in his thesis, *The Church in the Philippines at a Turning Point of its History*, notes how this folk Catholicism has continued and persisted over these four centuries:

> Toward the Spanish clergy the Filipinos agreed on an informal conspiracy of silence to keep the religious (leaders) ignorant of the continuation of clandestine pagan rituals, practice, and beliefs. The conspiracy of silence on the part of the *Indios* (tao) and of *fiscales* (supervisors of catechetical instruction) contributed to the Filipinization of Christianity, a syncretistic form of Christianity, a blending of Christian elements with belief in spirits (1972:18).

As we will see later, the same "informal conspiracy of silence" exists today between church members of all Christian groups and their church leaders.

## Adjusting the framework

Despite these differences in areas of concern and this "conspiracy of silence," there are areas in which Roman Catholicism and animism overlap. These areas involve the use of religious statues and revered objects for worship, blessings, the use of "holy water," and praying to saints. All of these areas fit quite nicely into the animistic framework of the Filipino with only slight adjustments. Local spirits were replaced with patron saints of the *barrio*. The crucifix was given the power and qualities of the animistic amulet. The palm leaves made into the shape of a cross which was blessed on Palm Sunday could ward off evil spirits when placed over the door of the house. Even today, most jeepneys, buses, and taxis have a small "shrine" with a statue of either the Virgin Mary or the *Santo Niño* (Jesus as child-king), with the belief that these objects will protect their travel.

Nowhere is this overlap more apparent than in the relationship between the living and their recently-dead ancestors. The Roman Catholic doctrine of purgatory fits in comfortably with the animistic belief in the ongoing presence of a person's spirit after death. The belief is that the dead spirit must be at peace before he can go on to heaven. If he died a tragic or early death, his spirit must be appeased so that it does not linger on earth to bother those who are still living. This is done through *novenas* or masses performed on the anniversary of the death of the ancestor. A trip to any cemetery on All Souls' Day will find it completely full of Filipinos bringing food to be placed at the grave sites of their dead loved ones. They usually spend the whole day and even all night with their dead ancestors.

The Black Nazarene of Quiapo and the *Santo Niño* of Cebu are religious statues which are believed to have power to heal the sick and protect against spirits. These statues are believed to have power that can be transmitted to a handkerchief or other cloth when rubbed against these sacred objects. These handkerchiefs and pieces of cloth can be carried to the sick for healing or carried by a person to ward off evil spirits or any misfortune.

In Cebu City, old ladies are paid to dance the *Pit Señor* to gain the attention and favor of the *Santo Niño*. These women dance in front of the church of the *Santo Niño* with the candles purchased by their patrons. These candles are thought to be more powerful because they have gained the attention of the *Santo Niño*. In January of each year, there is a procession in which thousands of people from all over the country and the world come to dance the *Pit Señor* in honor of the *Santo Niño* of Cebu.

It is not difficult to see the animistic elements in the above beliefs and observances. In these areas where Roman Catholicism overlaps with animism, there is no apparent inconsistency seen by the individual or the church. Roman Catholicism and animism can coexist quite nicely together as long as each is fulfilling its separate functions.

Since the first baptism in Cebu by Magellan in 1521, until today, folk Catholicism remains the religion of the majority of the Filipinos.

## AMERICAN PROSTESTANTISM COMES TO THE PHILIPPINES

During the 377-year rule of Spain over the Philippines, Roman Catholicism was the official religion of the country. This ended when Spain ceded the Philippines to the United States in 1898, under the terms of the Paris Peace Treaty. In 1902, the Roman Catholic Church ceased to be the official religion of the Philippines, based on the American belief in the separation of religion and government (Anderson 1969:209).

This separation established a climate of religious freedom

which introduced different religious groups from within the Philippines and from the United States. The Philippine Independent Church (Aglipayan) was formed as a splinter group from the Roman Catholic Church (Demetrio 1981:112). In 1914, another indigenous church group emerged, the *Iglesia ni Kristo* (Anderson 1969:350). At the same time, Protestant missionaries under various mission boards began to arrive. These groups added a new dimension to the religious life of the Philippines (Neill 1982:345).

These Protestant missionaries were confronted with a vastly different religious situation than the one that confronted Magellan and the Roman Catholic clergy of the sixteenth century. The early Catholic clergy was charged with the task of evangelizing the "pagan" and "primitive" Filipinos. They were supposed to convert these people from animism to Roman Catholicism; but actually, the conversion was from animism to folk Catholicism. The Protestant missionaries, on the other hand, came to the Philippines to convert Roman Catholic Filipinos to Protestantism.

Yet, the difference may not be as great as one may assume at first thought. As was suggested before, Roman Catholicism became, for most Filipinos, their religion of ultimate concerns, leaving most of their animistic beliefs and practices untouched or little altered. Roman Catholicism replaced what the Filipino animists believed at the level of ultimate concerns, but not at the level of the practical everyday concerns. Protestantism, as brought to the Philippines by westerners, was also a religion of ultimate and higher concerns. It had no theology of weather, fishing, hunting, agriculture, or house building. Protestantism entered and competed with Roman Catholicism at the level of ultimate concerns only. When a person was converted to Protestantism he was converted at the level of ultimate concerns, leaving to the Filipino Protestant his everyday, practical religion which was animism. Thus a new religion was created, "folk Protestantism."

## A new "folk" religion

Folk Protestantism is a blend of Protestantism at the level of ultimate concerns (salvation, sin, forgiveness, heaven, and hell) and animism (a strong belief in the spirit world) at the level of everyday concerns. Folk Protestantism has a very different look than folk Catholicism. This is based more on a Protestant reaction to Roman Catholicism than on a reaction against animistic practices. Whereas Roman Catholicism is very willing to allow beliefs and practices which do not conflict with the teachings of the Catholic Church, Protestant missionaries, in general, have not been as permissive.

For example, the Roman Catholic Church allows and even encourages its members to bring palm branches to church on Palm Sunday. It is believed that the palm branches which are blessed during the mass on this day will have special powers to drive and keep away evil spirits from homes. Though this practice is not part of Roman Catholic theology, it is allowed by the Church since it does not contradict the other teachings.

On the other hand, Protestant missionaries are very concerned to guard the Church against any mixture of what would be termed "pagan" or "worldly" beliefs and practices. Protestants believe that the Church should allow only what the Bible explicitly says is permitted. Consequently, Protestant missionaries have always condemned such things as the use of religious statues or objects on the basis that they are or tend toward idolatry. There is no tolerance in the Protestant Church for any practice which has even the appearance of being animistic or pagan. There is also little tolerance for anything that has the appearance of being Roman Catholic.

Though Protestant missionaries are very concerned about the external signs of animism in the Filipino Protestant, they have had little or nothing to say to his animistic worldview. This is probably based on the assumption that Filipinos are purely Roman Catholic in their religion. Many Protestant missionaries believed that conversion to Protestantism and rejection of Catholicism changes the Filipino only at the level of ultimate concerns, and not at the animistic level.

So at the level of ultimate concerns, folk Catholicism and folk Protestantism share the same similarities and differences which exist between Roman Catholicism and Protestantism. At the animistic level, folk Catholicism and folk Protestantism differ in their external practices but share virtually the same spirit worldview.

A study of the western Christian worldview and the Filipino Christian worldview will help in understanding this religious blend called "folk Christianity."

# 2
# WESTERN AND FILIPINO WORLDVIEWS

It is a strange and wonderful fact that two cultures can observe the same world in different ways. This is certainly the case with western and Asian cultures which are greatly different from each other.

Cultures tend to pattern or program people's ways of perceiving things. These cultural patterns are the filters or maps with which the members of a given culture perceive the world around them. These concepts of reality which are generally agreed to by the members of a culture are called its "worldview" (Kraft 1979:53).

In order to better understand the folk Christianity of the Filipino it may be helpful to examine a generalization of a typical western Christian worldview in comparison with a typical Filipino Christian worldview. For this comparison we will use the model of the two-level and three-level worldviews espoused by Dr. Paul Hiebert in "The Flaw of the Excluded Middle" (1982).

## THE WESTERN CHRISTIAN WORLDVIEW: NATURAL AND SUPERNATURAL

The western Christian mind sees the universe divided into the natural and the supernatural. The natural category includes those things that are usually *this worldly* and come under the domain of the sciences, while in the supernatural category there is God (as a Trinity), Satan, angels and demons. All of these beings are *other worldly* spirit beings. Angels and demons are pretty much ignored, or seen as caring for the affairs of God and Satan in the *other worldly* realm. Virtually all systematic theologies deal with the subjects of angels and demons, but westerners feel these have little or nothing to do with the affairs of the Christian. So the existence of angels and demons is not denied, rather, it is ignored. This leaves the average western Christian with very little knowledge about angels and demons.

God is seen as holy and different from man. He is all-knowing (omniscient), all-powerful (omnipotent), all-present (omnipresent), and all-loving (gracious). Most western Christians see Satan as having many of the same abilities and powers which God possesses, using them for his own evil designs which are contrary to God and man.

Today, western Christianity largely ignores the existence of a spirit world which is *other worldly*. This was not always the case. The disappearance of this realm of the spirit world (the "excluded middle") is a rather recent event in Christian history. Its elimination came to the West in the same way that this category of the spirit world is being challenged today in the Philippines through scientific education.

For thousands of years the people of God (first the children of Israel and then the Church) have believed and interacted with *this worldly* spirit world. From the visit to Abraham by three angels in Genesis, to the vision of myriad of angels to John in the Book of Revelation, we see man in relationship to a spirit world. The Bible is also full of accounts of people who were practitioners of the spirit world.

The Christian Church has always believed in the existence of a spirit world populated by angels and demons. The practitioners who used the power of demons were called witches. The belief in witches and their power was almost universal for the first 1,700 years of Christianity (Gluckman 1972:274). Even such men as Thomas Aquinas concluded that witchcraft was real and witches received their power from Satan. In America in 1692, twenty alleged witches were executed for witchcraft. The belief in the ability of the living to contact spirits of the dead and other spirits was very popular in the United States. In 1857, a list of sixty-seven books and magazines on spiritualism was included in the *Practical Christian*. Beliefs in spiritualism and the existence of a *this worldly* spirit world was widespread in America (Sweet 1975:280).

As America moved into the twentieth century, there was a rising interest in everything "scientific." This had its effects on the church, especially Protestantism. William W. Sweet in his book, *The Story of Religion in America*, says,

> After World War I there was much talk of the scientific approach to religion and the scientific religion was much extolled from the pulpit. Those were the days when every branch of learning tried some sort of tie-up with the word science. It was indeed a charmed word (1975:419).

Science increasingly attempted to abolish anything that was supernatural. This affected the church in varying degrees.

The effect that science has on most Christians in America is that they desire a Christianity that is compatible with science. American Christians seem to have reached a compromise with science. They will leave the natural world to the domain of science, and the ultimate concerns of salvation and eternal life to Christianity. Though these areas of ultimate concerns cannot be proven scientifically, neither can they be disproved. In this way, we have excellent scientists who are also Christians. As scientists of this world, they would accept nothing by faith. As Christians, they accept the ultimate concerns by faith because they belong to a category which is *other worldly*. This compromise leaves the American Christian his religion of ultimate concerns while maintaining intellectual credibility.

However there is no place in this Christian-Scientific compromise for talk of a spirit world that is *this worldly*. Spirit world talk that is *this worldly* conflicts with explanations of science which are also *this worldly*. Science has clearly won in this conflict. For the western mind, spirits do not exist because everything *this worldly* has perfectly logical and natural (scientific) explanations. To believe in the existence of this spirit world would bring on judgments of ignorance and superstition and make a person's intellectual credibility suspect.

American Christian theology has indeed undergone a great deal of change in the past few decades. In fact William Sweet states,

> At no period in the history of American Christianity has there been more rapid change in the theological scene than has been witnessed within the past generation. The principal reason for this fact is the radical revolutionary changes which have been taking place in the whole political, economic, social and religious climate of the world. For after all, theology is not final truth handed down from above, but grows out of man's condition; it comes out of a human background (1975:417).

The impact of this change in western theology is certainly felt in the area of the spirit world. Many western Christians find it hard to believe in angels and demons. Though angels are mentioned from Genesis to Revelation, western Christians tend to ignore this category of spirit world beings. Dealing with demons was a very important part of the ministry of Jesus, but westerners have explained these occurrences as being of a psychological, and not a spiritual nature.

Angelology and demonology is a part of the majority of systematic theologies but it is not a part of the worldview and practice of the western Christian. This leaves him with the categories of angels and demons which are not a part of his actual worldview or practice.

For scientific western Christians, any being, process or thing which is neither God, Satan, angels, nor demons (Roman Catholicism includes the Virgin Mary and saints) is in the category of the natural or believed not to exist. The things in the natural category can be explained or proven scientifically. Man in all his physiological and psychological processes is in the natural category and can be understood scientifically. All sickness is natural and can be explained and cured medically. The planting and harvesting of crops is natural and can be explained agriculturally.

However, *dwende* (a small spirit being which appears to its patron) cannot be explained nor proven — so to the average westerner it does not exist. Also *sigbin* (creatures with kangaroo-like features, said to jump from one island to another) do not exist, for the same reason. There is room in the supernatural or *other worldly* category of the westerner only for God, Satan, angels, demons, and nothing else.

## FILIPINO CHRISTIAN WORLDVIEW: NATURAL; SUPERNATURAL *THIS WORLDLY*, AND SUPERNATURAL *OTHER WORLDLY*

The typical Filipino Christian worldview has a natural, *this worldly* category which is very much like that of the western Christian though somewhat narrower in scope. However, it is in the supernatural realm where a greater difference between western and Filipino worldviews is found. The supernatural category of the westerner is basically *other worldly* in that it deals with ultimate concerns and contains God, Satan, angels and demons (also the Virgin Mary and saints for Roman

Catholics). The Filipino also has this same category of supernatural beings who are *other worldly* and take care of the ultimate concerns of salvation, sin, forgiveness, heaven and hell. But in addition to this category of the supernatural, the Filipino has a class of beings which are concerned with the more practical affairs of this world. This class of spirit being will be called *supernatural this worldly*.

| Western Worldview | Filipino Worldview |
|---|---|
| Supernatural — Natural<br>/<br>*other worldly* | Supernatural — Natural<br>/ \<br>*other worldly*   *this worldly* |

For the Filipino Christian, the *supernatural other worldly* category contains only God and Satan (and the Virgin Mary for Roman Catholics). Satan is seen as being much like God in terms of his power and abilities, though he does not have as much power as God. The power of God is used for His glory and for man's benefit while the power of Satan is used to hinder the plans of God and for man's harm. God is seen as a heavenly Father who is distant and unapproachable. He is, however, good, loving and concerned with man's ultimate destiny.

For the more practical affairs of everyday living, the Filipino believes that God is too "big" to be intimately concerned. So He has lesser spirit beings to handle these more pragmatic and mundane concerns (Sitoy 1969:61). For the Filipino this is the *supernatural this worldly* category. The population of this category is enormous. There is no sharp differentiation between the various beings in the *supernatural this worldly* category; they are all seen as merely "spirits." However, if pressed, most Filipinos would say that there are angels, demons, ancestral spirits and other types of spirit beings. There are varying degrees of power and abilities in these spirit beings; power is differentiated not between classes of spirit beings but within each class.

(The pre-Spanish Filipino belief in the existence of lesser "gods" has been lowered to the category of *this worldly* spirits).

## *This worldly* spirit beings

While angels, demons and ancestral spirits are all of the same "sort," there is another kind of spirit being in the *supernatural this worldly* category. Such a spirit being is the *dwende* who is a very small spirit-like person. The *dwende* can make himself visible, but usually does so only with a person with whom he has a relationship. The *dwende* protects this person from other elements of the spirit world as well as giving information about the future. On October 20, 1982, DYBU radio in Cebu City reported on their morning newscast the possible appearance of a *dwende* in the courthouse:

> The provincial courthouse was disrupted today by the presence of tiny footprints which had been left from the night before. These footprints were found on the clock and on the stenographer's table. The size of the footprints indicated that they belonged to either a *dwende* or a one-month old baby.

An *agta* or *capri* is an enormous spirit being who is normally invisible but who can make himself visible at will. Twice the size of a man, he lives in trees and can be either friendly or evil. A bright, highly educated woman described for me her "family ogre."

> George was our family ogre who lived in a tree near the house. He could hide the children for fun but more often he was called on to protect them while they played. We knew that he liked to sit under the house because he would leave a "print" of his bottom in the dirt where he had been sitting. He very much liked to tickle grandpa when he slept outside for siesta and to tease the family by turning on the lights in the middle of the night (Henry 1981:a).

In different regions of the country, people believe in some of these types of spirit beings.

Several people would tell of belief in one type of spirit being (like the *dwende*), and call superstitious another's belief in a different spirit being (such as *agta*). And there are many who would deny this group of spirit beings completely.

For the Filipino, there is no clear differentiation between the *this worldly* supernatural category and the natural category. There are beings which could belong in both of these categories. For example, witches who can be transformed from human into spirit beings. A *wakwak* is an evil female witch who detaches the upper part of her body from the waist. While hiding the lower half of her body (perhaps under the banana leaves) she can fly around doing her evil deeds which include satisfying her appetite for human internal organs. The sound she makes while flying is *"wakwak."* The *wakwak* is a *supernatural this worldly* being for the Filipino.

## THE RESULT OF THE CONFRONTATION OF WORLDVIEWS

The confrontation of worldviews has influenced the Filipino's way of looking at his world. Exposure to the western scientific model in education and religion has given another dimension to the Filipino worldview. The

> scientific explanation for things in the natural world has become more common for Filipinos, but they have accepted it on their own terms. Rather than always replacing their animistic explanations, science has often merely become another option for explaining natural phenomena (Healy 1984).

The Filipino Christian is increasingly facing the challenge of science to his supernatural worldview. However, this challenge is not coming to all parts of this culture at the same time because only a part of the society can avail itself of higher education, where this confrontation with science takes place. This leaves a society in which there is a great variation in terms of education and, therefore, variations in exposure to scientific knowledge and thinking.

These differences in educational level produce wide variations between spirit world explanations and scientific explanations in the minds of Filipinos. Some Filipinos are at the scientific end of the scale, some are at the spirit world end of the scale, and most are somewhere in the middle of the scale, blending scientific and spirit world explanations.

Even within the mind of an individual Filipino there will be both scientific explanations and spirit world explanations. As science confronts the spirit world explanations, science can replace them, be added to them, or be rejected by the spirit world explanations.

## Replacing spirit world explanations with science

Confrontation with the western scientific worldview in western Christianity as well as western education has caused a reduction in the population of the *this worldly supernatural* category for many Filipinos.

Prior to their confrontation with western science, Filipinos believed that the weather was controlled by spirits. Rituals and sacrifices were used to control the spirits of the weather.

Today, however, there would be few Filipinos who would believe that spirits are in control of the weather. Weather has been explained scientifically so that there is no longer a need for the Filipino to explain this "mystery" in terms of the spirit world. The scientific explanation is believed instead of the spirit world explanation.

## Adding science to spirit world explanations

There are areas of animistic belief which have not been destroyed by scientific explanations. Rather, the scientific explanation is believed in addition to the animistic explanation. This is the case with the explanation of sickness and healing. Medicine believes it has an explanation for sickness which is scientific. Filipinos would not deny that explanation for many sicknesses. However, most Filipinos believe that this medical explanation is not complete because it does not include sickness which can be caused by the spirit world. These sicknesses caused by the spirit world cannot be cured by western medicine; their cure must come from those who practice spirit world medicine.

When a Filipino gets sick he asks three questions which reveal the three sources of sickness from his point of view. First, he asks: "What is the physical cause of this sickness?" After years of western education and medicine, he knows that there are physical causes for illness. It could be something that he ate or drank, a change in the weather, taking a bath at the wrong time (during menstruation or fever), or germs. For these sicknesses, he goes to the doctors. In the major cities, medical doctors are some of the best in the world, with virtually all specialists available. However, due to the cost of this western medicine and its inaccessibility in rural areas, many do not avail of its services.

Though western medicine is not available to many of the people, folk medicine is. Folk medicine includes a wide range of specialists from those who use only herbs and chemicals to those who mix medicine with the use of spirit world powers. The folk practitioner may diagnose the problem and provide a cure which could include both herbs (medicine) and saying a powerful prayer.

In an interview with a close friend from the island of Siquijor, a good example of the use of a folk practitioner for healing was given.

> My grandfather had been very sick for weeks. His problem appeared to be constipation. We took him to the doctor but he did not get any relief. So we decided to take him to a local "quack doctor." The "quack doctor" told my grandfather to kill one of the nearby chickens and to examine the intestines of that particular chicken. My grandfather did as he was told and found that that particular chicken which he had killed had a piece of string tied around its intestine such that the intestines were blocked. The "quack doctor" told him to untie the string and that he would be relieved of his problem. My grandfather untied the string on the intestines of the chicken and he was soon relieved of his problem (Henry 1982:a).

The use of the term "quack doctor" by the Filipino in this interview shows a part of the ambivalence that the Filipino has in dealing with these practitioners. He may refer to them in negative terminology, yet might still go to them in times of crisis or illness.

The second question that the Filipino asks when sick, especially if there is no apparent physical cause or if medical doctors are not able to cure him, is: "What have I done to get this sickness?" Behind this question is the belief that if God or the spirit world has been offended, then sickness could be sent as a punishment. With the influence of western Christianity at the level of ultimate concerns having such an emphasis on the concept of sin, the Filipino naturally sees sickness as a punishment from God for his sin. Then the process of appeasing God begins. The first step in dealing with sickness that is seen as punishment for sin is forgiveness and penance. Forgiveness from God is dealt with somewhat differently by Protestants and Roman Catholics, but in either case it is the initial step.

The next stage in dealing with illness as punishment is to attempt to appease God by promising Him something regarding the future. "Lord, if you will just take away this sickness from me (or my child, or my wife), then I will..." What the person promises to do for God depends on what he thinks it will take in order for God to answer his prayer. It may be a promise to stop sinning, a promise to go into full-time Christian ministry, a promise to give money to the church, or a promise to be a better Christian by attending church more often. This is a kind of bargaining with God which is based on the animistic assumption that man can get his way with God if he knows what God wants.

The third question which a Filipino asks regarding his sickness is: "Who did this to me?" There is a predominant belief that practitioners of the spirit world (a *mananambal* or a *mangkukulam*) can bargain with the spirit world to send sickness to other people. These practitioners or sorcerers can be hired for the purpose of inflicting spirit world sickness on another.

Of the many types of spirit-caused sicknesses, the most often mentioned is a sickness which is caused by sorcery or witchcraft. One such practitioner of the spirit world is called a *barangan* (Lieban 1967:50). The *barangan* uses his relationship with the spirit world as well as "special" insects to send sickness to any one he so chooses. The *barangan* is usually employed by a person who wants "justice" (revenge) on another person. Once a person has a *barang* sickness, western medicine is said to be powerless against it. The cure can only come from one who knows counter-sorcery. This *mananambal* also has a relationship with the spirit world and can find out what to do to bring about a cure. It may be necessary to find a *mananambal* who has more power than the *barangan* who inflicted the sickness before a cure can be obtained.

There is a very interesting account from Mindanao in which a man took his brother to a *mananambal* to determine if the sickness he had was the result of a *da-ut* (another spirit-caused curse of sickness which is the result of sorcery). The sick brother had been to three hospitals but was not getting any better, so he was taken to a *mananambal*, who was a practitioner of the spirit world for healing and casting out spirits:

> The *mananambal* took one of the small Añejo rum bottles (the small pocket-size) and put some *lana* (coconut oil) and some other medicine in it. He placed the bottle between his legs with the narrow edge pointing up. He then took a regular chicken and egg and placed it on the edge of the bottle. He told my brother to name all of the people who might have wanted to put a *da-ut* on him. He said that if my brother's sickness was *da-ut*, the egg would stand on end on the narrow edge of this bottle. My brother named everyone he could think of that could possibly have done this. In the meantime, the *mananambal* was trying to balance the egg on the edge of the bottle but it wouldn't balance. This was to be the sign that the sickness was not a *da-ut*. The *mananambal* said that he should do it again because he felt that it really was a sickness caused by a *da-ut*. As my brother came to one name, the egg continued to stand on end while he talked about how his son had eloped with the daughter of that woman. But when they returned, he had refused to allow them to marry and sent his son to

Manila where he finally married someone else. The *mananambal* was sure that it was *da-ut* and went about curing the sickness through counter-sorcery (Henry 1980).

There is another spirit world sickness, called *buyag* in Cebuano, which is the result of sorcery or witchcraft (Lieban 1977:71). This sickness can come directly from the spirit world if a person offends a spirit by hitting it when throwing something out of the window, by violating an enchanted place or in many other ways. Or the sickness can come from the spirit world indirectly as a curse given by another person. This curse can be given by a person in the form of a compliment which is then reversed by the spirit world into a curse of sickness. A person who is always giving curses through compliments is a *buyagan*. The curse can be avoided by complimenting the *buyagan* before he compliments you or your children, thus rendering his curse powerless.

The cure for *buyag* is *tut-ho*, given to the patient by a person called a *manunut-ho*. The *manunut-ho* chews a special combination of leaves and then spits the leaves on the area of the body which is affected by the *buyag* in order to cure the patient.

Finally, there is a sickness called *hilo* which has a physical cause, but a spirit world cure. Many Cebuano Filipinos expressed fear of *hilo*. *Hilo* is a poison which is put into the food of an unsuspecting person to cause sickness or death (Lieban 1977:54). The sorcerer who uses this poison is called *hilo-an*. He is said to be able to hide the *hilo* under his fingernails and put it into the food or drink of a person he wishes to harm or kill. One family in Leyte related how they must constantly stand guard on their food, specially at fiesta time, to protect the family from *hilo*. The *hilo-an* can be employed by an enemy of a person for revenge or other reasons. The cure for *hilo* can be divined by a *mananambal* or by another *hilo-an*.

The confidence put in the scientific cure of the animistic cure for sickness varies from person to person. Sickness and its cure are examples where the scientific explanation was simply added to the animistic explanation and did not completely replace it.

## Rejecting science in favor of the spirit world explanation

One area of animistic belief which has gone virtually untouched by science is divination. Divination attempts to give a person information which would not be available to him by ordinary means. This could be information about something or someone in which only the spirit world could know or find out. Or this information could be about the future. The diviner is a spirit world practitioner who specializes in getting information from the spirit world. The spirits may communicate to him directly in a voice audible to him or they may speak through the diviner to others who are present. The spirits can also choose to communicate through scores of devices which can be used by a diviner. Diviners or fortune-tellers can "read" such devices as tarot cards, crystal balls, tea leaves at the bottom of the cup, the bumps on a person's head, his handwriting, the palm of his hand. The liver or other internal organs of animals, or the stars and planets can also be used. But the basic idea is that the diviner has ways in which the spirit world communicates with him so that he can give, or more likely sell, the information to others.

It is difficult to think of divination as animistic because it is so widespread around the world. For even to the most scientific person, it is difficult to leave so many of life's decisions to chance or luck. That is why so many people the world over go to these practitioners of the spirit world to get information in order to make seemingly better and wiser decisions.

In the Philippines and around the world, diviners of various sorts are consulted about things in every area of life:

> A diviner once described to me the person who stole some things out of my house. And from that description I knew exactly who he was talking about (Henry 1981:b).
>
> In my first visit to a diviner, he told me my occupation and the fact that I had only one child and could not have any more (Henry 1982:b).
>
> The diviner told me that I would soon be having another child. I thought that impossible since I was beyond child-bearing age. A short time later my husband confronted me with the need for adopting a child (Henry 1981:c).
>
> I consult with a diviner on every major business transaction to make sure I am doing the right thing. I even ask him about the best days for making the deals (Henry 1982:d).
>
> Our diviner said that our son's fiancée would be a very good wife for our son and so we gave him our permission to get married (Henry 1983).

In the Philippines, there are many classes of diviners as well as many types of devices employed. In the cities among the educated, the diviners are used in matters of business and investment. The information given by the diviner helps the person to reduce his anxiety about these matters by feeling that the decisions are not left to chance but are based on information from the spirit world. Other diviners give fishermen, hunters and farmers the information that they need to help reduce anxiety in making decisions related to their needs.

Divination is a spirit world process and not a scientific process. Science ridicules even the possibility of providing information about the future from spirits or stars. Yet, science has not been able to challenge the spirit world in this area of divination for most Filipinos.

## SPECIALIZATION: A RESULT OF WORLDVIEW CONFLICT

The confrontation of worldviews has had its effect on the church. Because the church in the Philippines has strong western influence it is more of a reflection of the western worldview than the Filipino worldview. The church is seen to "specialize" in matters of ultimate concern. But the church does not incorporate the total belief system of the Filipino. The animistic belief and practices which "specialize" in everyday concerns must be added to this to make it the total belief system of the Filipino. Therefore, worldview conflict has caused specialization among practitioners of the supernatural.

It will be shown that there is a great deal of specialization in the belief and practice systems of Filipino folk Christianity. There are those who are the *in-church* practitioners who specialize in the *other worldly* spirit beings and the ultimate concerns (the nature of God, sin, salvation, forgiveness, heaven and hell). This leaves the *out-of-church* practitioners to deal with the *this worldly* spirit world which involves the more everyday concerns of the Filipino.

### *In-church* practitioners

The Protestant pastor and the Roman Catholic priest are the practitioners of the *other worldly supernatural* category. They are specialists in the matters of ultimate concerns. They are often seen as the mediators between God and man. They teach others about what God wants and pray to God on behalf of their members. These practitioners of ultimate concerns lead the people in rituals of ultimate concern which are called worship service (Protestant) or masses (Roman Catholic). This entire belief and ritual system of ultimate concerns is organized into the institution which is called the "church."

Within the institution of the church there are those who further specialize in specific areas of ultimate concern. There is the theologian who specializes in organizing and writing the belief systems or doctrines of the church. There are evangelists who specialize in the area of salvation. And there are those whose specialty is pastoral care or meeting the ultimate concern needs of the members.

## *Out-of-church* practitioners

There are also *out-of-church* practitioners who avail themselves of *this worldly supernatural* powers. These people are the mediators between man and the spirit world. They deal with people where the spirit world meets the everyday life of the Filipino (sickness, divination, fertility, fishing, agriculture, business and investments).

There is a loose institution of these *out-of-church* practitioners which is very informal. Some are members of spiritist groups while others meet informally with other practitioners in their area to trade ideas and secrets. Though practising these "magical arts" is against the formal laws of the Philippines, nothing is done to enforce those laws. It would be impossible to force *out-of-church* practitioners to stop their business because it is such an integral part of the Filipino worldview.

Anthropologists call these people who work with the spirit world "shaman." In Cebuano they are called *mananambal* and they are the general practitioners of the spirit world (Lieban 1967:27), The English translation of this word reflects the western bias and evaluation of this type of spirit world practitioner. The word *mananambal* is translated in English as "quack doctor" by westerners and western-influenced and educated Filipinos. For a westerner, a quack doctor is a person who has no knowledge or ability to cure.

These spirit world practitioners also specialize in various areas of their work. They are therefore called by what they can do and the methods which they employ. In Zamboanga, a shaman or spirit world practitioner who specializes in finding lost articles, animals or people is called a *mananagan*. In the mountains near Cebu City the shaman who specializes in sorcery (putting curses on people) is a *mangkukulam*. The *manunut-ho* specializes in removing sickness which is the result of *buyag* (a curse from the spirit world). There are practitioners of the spirit world who use a type of "supernatural" massage for healing fractures and other ailments of the bones, joints, and muscles called *manghihilot*. The names of these spirit world practitioners and the methods that they use vary from region to region but they make themselves available to people for these and other specialized purposes related to the more common and everyday needs and concerns of Filipinos.

These shamans or *mananambal* get their power for both diagnosis and healing from mentor spirits. These spiritual benefactors which give the *mananambal* his power claim to be spirits of a deceased *mananambal*, saints, the Virgin Mary, Christ or God (Lieban 1977:30).

The mentor spirits provide for the *mananambal* some very important help and information for healing and diagnosis. This information is given to them in dreams, visions, or impressions. One *mananambal* related to the author how he would be given information about a patient "from an old man with a long white beard." The information would include both the diagnosis and the cure for the patient. The spiritual benefactors of the *mananambal* provide the power that is necessary to back up their cure. The spirit world provides for the shaman both information and power in order to diagnose and cure sickness (Lieban 1977:31).

There is ritual associated with the practitioners of the *this worldly supernatural* category. In many ways, these rituals are much more formal and strict than the ritual of the practitioners of the *other worldly supernatural* category (priests and pastors). For pastors and priests, the power is not as much in the ritual itself as in God, the object of the ritual. For the *mananambal* the power exists in both the spirit world and in the ritual itself. The precise execution of the ritual is a display to the spirit world that the shaman is trusting them to perform or communicate for them. For the *mananambal* there is power in the words spoken, the devices used, and even the time in which the ritual is performed. All of these things are done in order to manipulate, obligate, or control the spirit world. The basis of animism is the belief that man can know the right "formulas" and rituals and, therefore, manipulate or control the spirit world to perform on his behalf.

As there is conflict between western and animist worldviews, so there is conflict between the practitioners of these worldviews. But, in the mind of the Filipino, each serves to meet a need not being met by the other.

## CONSPIRACY OF SILENCE: A RESULT OF WORLDVIEW CONFLICT

One of the most obvious results of this conflict of worldviews is that Filipinos have become very reluctant to discuss the spirit world openly with westerners for fear of being labeled as "ignorant and superstitious." For this reason, there still exists today what has been described as an "informal conspiracy of silence." This "informal conspiracy of silence" exists between church members and church leaders of the Protestant and the Roman Catholic Church. (It also exists between students and educational leaders.) The following interview with a

Filipino pastor reveals why the "conspiracy of silence" is still in existence today.

> I received a letter from a woman teacher in a theological school which asked me to come to the school immediately. She explained that one of the students was being "troubled by demons," and she wanted me to come to the school to handle the situation. I decided that I would go. On the way to the school, I stopped to ask our American missionary to pray for me and for the situation with the student. When I explained the situation to him, he simply laughed at me and changed the subject. That was the last time I ever talked to an American about the spirit world (Henry 1982:c).

Although few in church circles are talking about the spirit world, it has been a very integral part of the Filipino worldview, and much has remained untouched by western thought and influence.

## WORLDVIEW CONFLICT: CONCLUSION AND CHALLENGE

Science, with its accompanying technology, is increasingly shrinking the *this worldly supernatural* category of the Filipino. Science explains natural phenomena in ways that replace the old belief that nature is in control of the spirit world. For the Filipino, more and more of the world is no longer under the domain of religion but is explained and controlled scientifically.

The significance attached to either the *this worldly supernatural* category or the natural category varies from Filipino to Filipino depending on his exposure to scientific explanations (western education). There are Filipinos who have been virtually untouched by modern scientific explanations and, therefore, explain much of life in terms of the *this worldly supernatural* category. On the other hand, there are Filipinos who have had intensive exposure to scientific explanations in the western style educational system of the Philippines. This confrontation between animism and science has resulted in the replacement of many areas of the *this worldly supernatural* category with natural or scientific explanation. This is not true, however, in the areas of sickness and divination which persist in the *this worldly supernatural* category in the minds of most Filipinos today.

The confrontation of Filipino folk Christianity with the western scientific worldview has generally reduced the significance of animism in areas of everyday life for many Filipinos. The western Christianity brought to the Philippines denies the existence of the spirit world as Filipinos know it. Western Christianity believes in a supernatural world which deals mainly with the ultimate concerns of salvation, sin, forgiveness, heaven, and hell. Everything that cannot be related to God and Satan either does not exist, or it is given a scientific explanation. In spite of this, animism is significant in Filipino thinking in areas of sickness, sorcery, and divination.

Folk Christianity is the total belief system of the Filipino which includes the ultimate concerns of the *other worldly supernatural* spirit world as well as the everyday concerns of the *this worldly supernatural* spirit world. Both, the *this worldly* and the *other worldly* aspects of Filipino folk Christianity have those who specialize in the spirit world.

It is the thesis of this book that the spirit worldview of the Filipino is compatible with the spirit worldview of the Bible. Both the Filipino spirit worldview and the worldview of the Bible believe that there are *this worldly* spirits which interact with man and nature.

This does not mean, however, that all the beliefs and practices of the Filipino regarding the spirit world are compatible with the Bible. The following chapters will examine the biblical data on the spirit world. Though there is a great deal of variety in the spirit world, it will be shown that spirits are first grouped together as to their loyalty. Those spirit beings loyal to God will be grouped under the "angelic" spirit world while those loyal to Satan will be grouped under the "demonic" spirit world.

The challenge of this book is to Filipinize the church. This is a challenge to return to the Bible to develop a theology of the spirit world. It is not a challenge to destroy a belief in the existence of a *this worldly* spirit world. Rather, it is a call to make the beliefs and practices of the Filipino spirit world compatible with the Bible and with the Christian's relationship with God. Filipinizing the church will require an examination of the Bible regarding the *this worldly* spirit world. It will then require an examination of the experiences and traditions which are believed regarding the spirit world in light of what the Bible says.

# 3
# THEOLOGICAL FOUNDATIONS: THE GOD AMONG SPIRITS

In a vast world of spirits, there exists a spirit being who is unlike any other spirit being. All spirit beings were created by this one, unique Spirit. So all spirit beings have a beginning, but the Creator Spirit has no beginning; He is eternal. Besides creating a vast spirit world, the Creator Spirit called into being out of nothingness the universe in which humans live.

In the midst of this spirit world and material universe, the Creator Spirit formed a being — man — to love. Now He had a being with whom He could have a relationship. He knew that man would need to be like Him, so He created man in His likeness. Now there would be a relationship based on love. The Creator Spirit had a unique relationship with man because only man had the image of His spirit.

Man enjoyed a wonderful situation in relation to both the Creator Spirit and the environment. The Creator Spirit knew all about him and his environment because He was the One who created it all. And man knew the Creator Spirit because the Creator loved him and walked and talked with him.

The Creator Spirit created man to exercise responsibility toward the rest of creation. Man was to be the caretaker of the earth. Besides being responsible for the environment, man was also given responsibility in his relationship with the

Creator Spirit. Since the Creator Spirit had created man, then man had a responsibility to Him to be obedient and not rebellious to His desires. The Creator Spirit would know everything and, therefore, would know what was best for man and the rest of the universe.

## The rebellion of the lying spirit

But all was not well in the spirit world which the Creator Spirit had made. The spirit world was created to give glory to the Creator Spirit and to minister to man's needs. In the beginning there was harmony and everything was very good. But one of the leading spirits which He had made was really a lying spirit. The lying spirit had lied to himself and to other spirits saying that he was equal with the Creator Spirit. It was true that the Creator Spirit had created him as a beautiful and powerful spirit, but he was not, nor ever would be, equal with the Creator Spirit.

This lying spirit caused a rebellion in the spirit world which led the Creator to cast him and his followers down to earth. One-third of the spirit world was loyal to the lying spirit and was cast down to earth to await further judgment from the Creator Spirit.

Meanwhile, in the physical realm of earth, the Creator Spirit had a wonderful relationship with man, the only being that He loved. Man was obedient to the Creator Spirit and the Creator Spirit loved and cared for him.

The lying spirit was angry with the Creator Spirit. He was not powerful enough to attack the Creator Spirit so he set out to hurt the Creator Spirit by destroying His relationship with man.

## The lying spirit deceived man

One day, the lying spirit took possession of a snake by entering its body and controlling its faculties. In this form, man did not recognize him as the lying spirit. The snake told man that there was no need to obey the Creator Spirit. He said that the Creator Spirit wanted obedience because He was afraid that man would be like Him. It was very tempting for man to rebel against the Creator Spirit, especially when he thought that he might become like the Creator Spirit or even equal with Him. This was, of course, the same lie that the lying spirit had used to cause rebellion in the spirit world. Unfortunately, man believed the same lie.

The result was that man lost his relationship with the Creator Spirit. The Creator Spirit had warned man not to rebel against His authority, but man believed the lying spirit instead of Him. With the relationship lost, each new generation of man would be born without the natural relationship with the Creator.

Consequently, man became concerned only with himself and not with the Creator Spirit. In fact, man was only conerned with himself as an individual and was not even concerned with his fellow man. This resulted very quickly in man murdering his brother. And the earth became a wicked place.

The lying spirit was in rebellion against the Creator Spirit, and so was man. In spite of man's rebellion, the Creator Spirit still loved him and wanted to bring him back into a relationship with Him. But man became wicked and evil. So the Creator Spirit destroyed man except for one family who was obedient to Him.

## Towards a restored relationship

The Creator Spirit chose a man with whom He would work to make Himself known. Through this man and his descendants, He would make a people who would be obedient and with whom He could have a relationship. Through this man he would teach the world that the Creator Spirit desired a relationship with man based on His terms. Man must put his complete trust and confidence in the Creator Spirit. This restored relationship would be based on faith.

The Creator Spirit chose to establish this faith relationship with man and his descendants. They became a mighty people because they were a people in right relationship with Him. The Creator Spirit gave these people a land in which to dwell. He gave them a law to show them what would please Him, and He sent spirit beings who were loyal to Him to minister to His people.

At times, these people would rebel against Him and believe the lies of the lying spirit. But the Creator Spirit would forgive their rebellion and disobedience if they showed a desire to have their relationship with Him restored. Man could show his desire to restore the relationship by sacrificing an animal and shedding its blood. This act showed the Creator Spirit that man was sincere and wanted the faith relationship restored.

The history of this people is a history of broken relationships with the Creator Spirit. Instead of becoming a humble people under His authority, they became proud. They believed that they were His special people because of their birth and not their faith. The lying spirit had convinced man that he did not need a relationship with the Creator Spirit. The people of the Creator Spirit were in a terrible condition because they had lost the meaning of their relationship. They had lost their faith.

## Creator Spirit on earth — Creator Man

The situation was so bad that the Creator Spirit did something that had never been done before. His plan for man was so unique and yet so perfect that only He Himself could accomplish it — the Creator Spirit came to earth personally to take charge of the situation.

The Creator of the universe came to earth in a very unexpected way. He came as a baby. And though He was still the Creator Spirit, He was also a man. The Creator Spirit took upon Himself human flesh, in all its limitations, and lived among men. He was then the Creator Man. Creator Man did this so that man could get an idea of what the Creator Spirit was like. He would also set the perfect example for man to follow in his relationship to Him as Creator Spirit. While on earth the Creator Man showed his absolute power over the lying spirit and those loyal to him by driving them away from the presence of man. But more importantly, the Creator Man demonstrated to man, once and for all, how much He loved him and wanted a relationship with him that was based on faith. Any man who had such a trust relationship with the Creator Spirit would enjoy this relationship for eternity. Physical death would lead to a continuation of this same eternal relationship.

Though the Creator Spirit could have come to earth as a king or ruler, He came as the son of a virgin and lived the simple life of a carpenter's son. After thirty years He started His mission on earth as Creator Man. Immediately upon starting this mission, He was met with the forces of the lying spirit who tried their best to tempt the Creator Man away from His mission. But they were not successful.

While he was on earth the Creator Man did not hesitate to suspend the normal workings of nature in order to show His love for man. He suspended nature in healing the sick, in quieting the storm, in raising the dead, and in feeding thousands of people from small amounts of food. The people called these things "miracles," but it was easy for the Creator of nature to suspend it at His will.

Creator Man was compassionate. He became intimately involved in the lives of man. He taught them truths regarding man's ultimate concerns, but he was also involved in man's everyday concerns. He felt all the things that man felt: fatigue, hunger, thirst, and even anger.

## Creator Man's sacrifice

At age thirty-three the time had come for the Creator Spirit, as Creator Man, to demonstrate His love for the world. He would do this by allowing Himself to be offered as a sacrifice and die like a common criminal. The Creator Man had spent His life demonstrating His love for man by calling man to have a relationship with Him. He died so that man might not be separated from Him for eternity.

Three days after His death came the most powerful demonstration of His ability to suspend nature. He defeated death by coming back to life. This was man's assurance that the Creator Spirit could keep His promise of eternal life for those who put their confidence in Him. After He came back to life He appeared to and talked with those who loved Him. He said to them that He would have to return to the Creator Spirit but that the Creator Spirit would return in another form so that they would not be alone.

The Creator Spirit told them that when He returned in this different form, they would be given power. With this power from the Creator Spirit, they would be able to perform wonderful works and also live in a way pleasing to Him. He kept this promise to those who trusted Him by faith. At a special festival time, He returned to earth as the indwelling Creator Spirit who would take possession of any person who would invite Him to enter his heart. This indwelling relationship would be based on man's belief that the death of the Creator Man was all that was necessary to restore this lost relationship.

## Creator Spirit lives in man by faith

Man can have a relationship with the Creator Spirit by having a form of the Creator Spirit living in him. The offer to be possessed by the indwelling Creator Spirit is still being made to man today. With the Creator Spirit in man, he will have power over the lying spirit. Once, man lived in fear because he lived under the shadow of the *this wordly* spirits and their leader, the lying spirit. Now man can exercise authority over these spirits because of the authority of the Creator Spirit who lives in him.

The Creator Spirit made a very special promise while He was here on earth as Creator Man. He promised that someday all of this rebellion on earth and in the spirit world would come to an end. He is going to bring this about by once again taking charge of the situation personally and returning to earth. This time He is going to come in judgment as the King of Kings and the Lord of Lords. Every knee will bow to Him and every tongue will confess that He is the Creator Spirit and Ruler of the universe. The lying spirit and all those who were loyal to him will be destroyed. Only those who have a loving relationship with the Creator Spirit based on faith will go into eternity with Him.

This is, of course, the message of Christianity. The heart of the Christian message is that God desires a loving relationship with man based on faith. Out of this relationship, God provides for man's ultimate concerns and He is intimate enough to desire to meet his everyday concerns as well. All Christian theology must be understood in light of the centrality of this relationship. The following examination of the spirit world will be made in light of the significance of the God/man relationship.

# 4
# THE ANGELIC SPIRIT WORLD

The reality of a Creator Spirit creating a spirit world is very difficult for the western mind to grasp. The western Christian can make allowances for a God in heaven (the *supernatural other worldly* category) who takes care of man's salvation from sin. But a spirit world (*supernatural this worldly* category) which exists in relationship to man and nature (natural category) is often doubted or denied by the western Christian with his scientific worldview. This denial began with eighteenth century Rationalism and today theologians speak of angels as merely symbolic beings.

> Eighteenth century Rationalism boldly denied the existence of angels and explained what the Bible teaches about them as species of accommodation. Some modern liberal theologians consider it worthwhile to retain the fundamental idea expressed in the doctrine of the angels. They find in it a symbolic representation of the protecting care and helpfulness of God (Berkhof 1939:143).

Filipinos have no such problem in believing in the existence of a spirit world. Filipinos see an enormous spirit world that coexists with the physical or natural world. This does not mean that they are ignorant of scientific explanation; for they are a bright and sophisticated people. It simply means that, for the Filipino, the scientific explanations apply to things in the natural category, but do not apply to a realm of *this worldly* spirit beings which interact with man (Hiebert 1982:42).

The confirmation of the existence of a *this worldly* spirit world does not come from any personal experience. Nor does the confirmation come because of the numerous interviews with Filipinos and westerners who have had firsthand experiences with the spirit world. The confirmation of the existence of *this worldly* spirit beings comes because the Bible says they exist and have dealings with man.

The existence of angels is an established biblical fact. The biblical concept of angels is broad and includes virtually all *this worldly* spirit beings. For the purposes of this discussion, however, we will separate angels into two major categories: those spirit beings which are loyal to God, which we will simply call angels, and those not loyal to God, which will be referred to as Satan and demons.

Angels are mentioned many times from Genesis to Revelation. Their ministry is to God directly and on behalf of God to man. So angels are spirit world beings who are both *this worldly*, in that they have dealings with man, and *other worldly*, in that they have dealings with God. The Bible may not tell us everything we want to know about angels and the spirit world, but it tells us everything that we need to know.

> From philosophy, therefore, we turn to Scripture, which makes no deliberate attempt to prove the existence of angels, but assumes this throughout, and in its historical books repeatedly shows us the angels in action. No one who bows to the authority of the Word of God can doubt the existence of angels (Berkhof 1939:143).

*Filipino Spirit World*

Although Christians bow to the authority of the Word of God concerning the existence of angels, the difficulty arises in the perception of these spirit beings. The Bible gives us an interesting story in 2 Kings 6:12-16. In this story, the king of Syria is going to Dothan to kill Elisha, the prophet. A servant of Elisha sees this army of the king of Syria surrounding the city of Dothan, in which he and Elisha are staying. This servant quickly runs in fear to Elisha to announce the terrible news, saying, "Alas, my master! What shall we do?" Elisha comforts the servant, "Do not fear, for those who are with us are more than those who are with them." The prophet was referring to angels or "chariots of fire." Elisha simply prayed that God would "open his eyes that he may see." God answered that prayer and the servant saw that they were surrounded by "chariots of fire" or angels, and not just by the enemy.

What is interesting is the fact that two men observing the same situation saw different things. Elisha saw angels, while the servant looked at the same thing and did not see the angels until God intervened. In the same situation, the angels were both visible and invisible depending on the observer. In the same way today, angels are both visible and invisible depending on the faith and openness of the observer, the circumstances, and the will of God.

The fact that westerners have trouble believing in angels and other spirit beings should in no way hinder such belief. The men of the Bible from Genesis to Revelation saw angels and had dealings with them. The history and religion of nearly all cultures show that they believed in the existence of "angelic" beings. And this is a belief that exists today in the Philippines.

This belief in angels was demonstrated when, on one occasion, there were about ten Filipino adults (mostly pastors) staying downstairs in our home. When they heard that we were awake the next morning, they all came upstairs to ask if

Camille, my wife, had been walking downstairs in the middle of the night. They had all seen someone dressed in a white robe walking around. When we said that none of us had gone downstairs all night, they suggested, without alarm or concern, that it must have been an angel.

## THE NATURE OF ANGELS

Perhaps the best understanding of the nature of angels will come in a comparison of angels with both God and man.

Scripture gives us some insight into the nature of angels, though a great deal must go unanswered on this matter. Discussion has gone on for centuries as to whether angels are purely spirit (with no bodies at all) or whether they have special bodies. These discussions bear little fruit. The Bible tells us that angels were created by God (Psalm 148:2-5), but their exact form is not known.

### Angels are spirits (Berkhof 1939:144)

The writer of Hebrews describes all angels as "ministering spirits" (Hebrews 1:14). This is certainly one distinction between angels and man. Because they are spirits, angels can be both visible and invisible depending on the will of God and the faith and openness of the individual to whom they reveal themselves.

### Angels surpass man in their knowledge

It was said to wise King Solomon,

> ...My lord is wise, like the wisdom of the angel of God, to know all that is in the earth.
>
> 2 Samuel 14:20

This text suggests that angels' knowledge and wisdom relates to earthly things. Angels have more knowledge than man, but they have their limits. Berkhof describes angels as, "while not omniscient, they are superior to men in knowledge" (1939:145). Jesus tells of His second coming and then says "But of that day or hour no one knows, not even the angels in heaven" (Mark 13:32). Strong agrees by saying,

> They are possessed of superhuman intelligence and power, yet an intelligence and power that has its fixed limits (1907:445).

## Angels are different from God

As spirits, angels would appear to be very different from man and more like God who is also a spirit (John 4:24). But to believe that angels are more like God than man would be to completely misunderstand the omnipotent, omniscient, omnipresent God of the Bible. Angels are spirit beings created by God to perform His will. They are not omnipresent though they are invisible. They are not omnipotent though they are powerful. They are not omniscient though they have more knowledge than man. The Bible says that man was created "a little lower than the angels" (Psalm 8:5 TLB). Angels are more like man than they are like God. However, they differ from man in their nature, power and knowledge.

## Angels: Their number and organization

In an interview for this book, a highly educated Filipino pastor said that he thought there would be at least as many spirits in the city of Cebu as there were people. The population of Cebu is approximately half a million. This seems like an outrageous overestimate until it is seen in light of what the Bible says in Revelation 5:11. Talking only of those spirits loyal to

God (angels) it says:

> And I looked, and I heard the voice of many angels around the throne and the living creatures and the elders; and the number of them was myriads of myriads, and thousands of thousands.

The King James Version reads "ten thousand times ten thousand." This passage tells of an angelic population in the millions upon millions. Even the psalmist writes about the number of angels when he writes in Psalm 68:17,

> The chariots of God are myriads, thousands upon thousands; the Lord is among them as at Sinai, in holiness.

Very little is known regarding the organization of these "hosts" of angels. One very good indication that there is a structure comes from the fact that Michael is called an archangel (Jude 9). This suggests that he is a high or chief angel. In all of Scripture only Michael is given this designation, which suggests that he is the angel of the highest rank (Revelation 12:7). The name Michael means "who is like unto the Lord."

The only other angel mentioned by name is Gabriel whose name means "God is great." The ministry of Gabriel occurs four times in the Bible. Each time he appears, he is bringing a message of good news. It was his privilege to announce to the Virgin Mary that she would have a child named Jesus. Though Gabriel is nowhere called an archangel, many believe that he is one because of the privileged tasks that he performed.

## SERAPHIM, CHERUBIM, AND OTHER STRANGE BUT WONDERFUL SPIRIT BEINGS

Seraphim are spirit world beings whose ministry is to give God praise, glory, and honor (Berkhof 1939:146). The description of these beings is certainly strange by most standards, but it must be remembered that the description comes from God's Word, the Bible.

> In the year of King Uzziah's death, I saw the Lord sitting on a throne, lofty and exalted, with the train of His robe filling the temple. Seraphim stood above Him, each having six wings; with two he covered his face, and with two ne covered his feet, and with two he flew. And one called out to another and said, "Holy, Holy, Holy, is the LORD of hosts, the whole earth is full of His glory."
> 
> Isaiah 6:1-3

This passage describes spirit beings with six wings. The phrase "one called out to another" suggests that there was more than one seraph. Since this is the only place in the Bible which describes seraphim, we do not know their exact number, power, or purpose. But from the above text we know that one of their tasks is to praise God by giving Him blessing, glory, and honor from their position above the throne of the God of the universe.

Cherubim are another strange but majestic and powerful sort of spirit being with wings. Like the seraphim, the cherubim are in the presence of God to give Him praise and adoration. While the seraphim perform their task above the throne of God, the cherubim perform theirs from below the throne.

> The Lord reigns, let the peoples tremble; He is enthroned above the cherubim, let the earth shake!
> 
> Psalm 99:1

The prophet Ezekiel describes the cherubim which he saw in a vision. This description of the cherubim is different from that of the seraphim though they are both winged spirit beings.

> These are the living beings that I saw beneath the God of Israel by the river Chebar; so I knew that they were cherubim. Each one had four faces and each one four wings, and beneath their wings was the form of human hands.
> Ezekiel 10:20,21

The four faces which Ezekiel tells about were previously described as the faces of a cherub, a man, a lion, and an eagle. So these spirit beings are given descriptions which are a combination of human and animal-like qualities.

> And within it there were figures resembling four living beings. And this was their appearance: they had human form. Each of them had four faces and four wings. And their legs were straight and their feet were like a calf's hoof, and they gleamed like burnished bronze. Under their wings on their four sides were human hands... As for the form of their faces, each had the face of a man, all four had the face of a lion on the right and the face of a bull on the left, and all four had the face of an eagle.
> Ezekiel 1:5 –10

Again, these cherubim are described in terms of animal-like qualities as well as human qualities. They were described as having a human form but "their feet were like a calf's hoof." The faces of these four "living beings" differ in that in Ezekiel 1, one of the faces of these beings is that of a bull, while in Ezekiel 10 it is a face of a cherub. This does not show a discrepancy in Scripture but it does show a variety in the spirit world.

There is good indication from Scripture that these winged cherubim are guardians of God's holiness. In the Garden of Eden, Adam and Eve were in the presence of God because they had not yet sinned. But after they had sinned, they were thrown out of the garden and God placed cherubim at the entrance to the garden so that they could not enter. Cherubim stood guard to protect God's holiness from the contamination of sin (Berkhof 139:147).

> So He drove the man out; and at the east of the garden of Eden He stationed the cherubim, and the flaming sword which turned every direction, to guard the way to the tree of life.
> Genesis 3:24

Cherubim were also on the ark of the covenant which was in the Holy of Holies of the tabernacle. The ark of the covenant was the symbol of God's presence with His people. Inside the ark of the covenant were placed the Ten Commandments (on tablets of stone), a golden jar of manna, and Aaron's rod, which budded. On top of the ark of the covenant was the mercy seat with two golden cherubim on either side. In this passage, the Lord speaks to Moses:

> And there I will meet with you, and from above the mercy seat, from between the two cherubim which are upon the ark of the testimony, I will speak to you about all that I will give you in commandment for the sons of Israel.
> Exodus 25:22

The suggestion here is that the cherubim's task is to protect the holiness of God. Only the High Priest could enter the Holy of Holies and only after he had been purified with the sacrificial blood. Once inside, the High Priest would be in the presence of God, who was above the mercy seat guarded by the two winged cherubim.

In the Revelation of John, one reads about "four living creatures" which surround the throne of God, giving Him constant praise. Their description is almost beyond human imagination. These creatures are similar yet different than those described by Ezekiel in his vision. The faces of these spirit beings are the same as those described in Ezekiel 1 but here there are six wings instead of four.

> And the first creature was like a lion, and the second creature like a calf, and the third creature had a face like that of a man, and the fourth creature was like a flying eagle. And the four living creatures, each one of them having six wings, are full of eyes around and within...
> Revelation 4:7,8

Certainly, there is variety in the angelic spirit world. God has at His disposal a vast and diverse spirit world, the description of which is beyond our comprehension as mere men. God created this diverse spirit world for the purpose of carrying out His will in heaven and on earth.

## THE MINISTRY OF ANGELS TO GOD

> Bless the LORD, you His angels,
> Mighty in strength, who perform His word,
> Obeying the voice of His word.
> Psalm 103:20

King David summarizes in this passage the ministry and purpose of angels as *other worldly* spirits. The text opens with an exhortation for the angels to "bless the Lord." This would certainly be a task which would come naturally from being in the presence of the Most High God. The text continues by saying that angels are God's possession. He created them and they belong to Him. Also note from the text that angels are "mighty in strength." As was previously suggested, angels are powerful spirit beings. Finally, Scripture says that angels are obedient to God and desire to do His will. "Thy will be done . . . as it is in heaven."

This, and similar passages (Job 38:7 and Revelation 5:11f), suggest that angels surround the throne of God and give Him praise.

## THE MINISTRY OF ANGELS TO MAN

> One reads here and there in Scripture that angels are celestial spirits whose ministry and service God uses to carry out all things He has decreed (e.g., Psalm 103:20-21). Hence, likewise, this name has been applied to them because God employs them as intermediary messengers to manifest Himself to men (Calvin 1977:165).

The desire and ability of angels to carry out the will of God sends them to man on behalf of God.

The ministry of angels to man as *this worldly* spirit beings must always be seen as an extension of their ministry to God. As members of the heavenly host, the primary direction of their gaze is toward God, not toward man (Adler 1982:11).

What angels do for man, they do under the guidance and direction of God. They are messengers and servants of God, created by Him. As created beings, angels should never be worshipped or prayed to. When the Apostle John made the mistake of falling in worship at the feet of an angel, he was sharply rebuked. The angel told him,

> Do not do it! I am a fellow servant with you and with your brothers the prophets and of all who keep the words of this book. Worship God!
>
> Revelation 22:9 NIV

As John was reminded, it is God alone who deserves our worship and praise.

Angels are not ministers of God's common grace to all mankind.

> Are they (angels) not all ministering spirits, sent out to render service for the sake of those who will inherit salvation?
>
> Hebrews 1:14

Apparently, it is only God's people who enjoy the ministry of God's angels.

Angels are sent by God to give service and help to His people as messengers, protectors, and spectators.

## Angels as messengers

God sends angels as messengers to man. In the Bible, this is by far the most common function of angels. From Genesis to Revelation, angels are sent by God to warn or bring good news to His people.

> That, by the way, is the literal meaning of the Hebrew and Greek words that become "angel" in English. Not all angels, as we shall see, serve as messengers, but the most frequent reference to them in Sacred Scriptures describes them as performing this mission (Adler 1982:11).

The biblical experiences of angels bringing messages to God's people are far too numerous to mention. It was an angel who stopped Abraham from sacrificing Isaac by showing him the ram to be sacrificed instead. An angel spoke to Moses in a burning bush as God told him that he would lead the children of Israel out of bondage. Angels were present when God wrote the Ten Commandments on the tablets of stone. Daniel was given a vision and message by an angel of what would happen to the world in the last days.

God continued to use angels as messengers as He unfolded His final plan of redemption in His Son, Jesus. It was God's plan to use John the Baptist to "prepare the way of the Lord." The good news of the birth of John was brought to Zacharias and Elizabeth by an angel.

> ... I am Gabriel, who stands in the presence of God and I have been sent to speak to you, and to bring you this good news.
>
> Luke 1:19

Likewise, the announcement of the birth of Jesus, to the Virgin Mary, was brought by the angel Gabriel. The good news of the birth of Christ was brought by angels to the shepherds who were in the fields.

The apostle Paul was ministered to by angels. His was a life of untold beatings and imprisonments until he was sent off to Rome to stand trial before Caesar. On his way to Rome with more than two hundred other passengers, he encountered a storm which threatened to wreck the ship. But an angel of the Lord appeared to Paul saying,

> Do not be afraid, Paul; you must stand before Caesar; and behold, God has granted you all those who are sailing with you.
>
> Acts 27:24

The angel's first words to Paul were "do not be afraid." Quite often angels created fear in the hearts of those to whom they appeared. But unless the angel comes in judgment, there is nothing to fear. It must be remembered that they are God's messengers who carry out God's will. Even after the death of Christ and the coming of the Holy Spirit at Pentecost, angels continue to be God's ministers of good news to His people.

Though angels are God's messengers of good news, they do not preach the gospel message of salvation to sinners. The task of evangelism has been given to man. However, God sends angels to aid man in evangelism. An example of this angelic aid is found in Acts 8:26, where an angel came to Philip with a message that he should go to the desert to a place called Gaza. Once there, Philip found an Ethiopian nobleman reading from the book of Isaiah. He joined the man and explained to him about the Scripture and about Jesus which resulted in the Ethiopian's salvation and baptism. The angel did not preach the message of salvation in Christ; he sent someone who could.

There is a similar situation which occurs in the book of Acts regarding Peter and Cornelius. In this account, an angel tells Cornelius to send for Peter who will give him the good news of salvation in Christ. Because Cornelius was a non-Jew (Gentile), Peter would not have even entered his house. But God gave him a vision to convince him that he must go and proclaim the good news of salvation. As a result, Cornelius was saved and baptized. It would have been much easier if the angel evangelized Cornelius. But the proclamation of the Good News is the task of man in the power of the Holy Spirit, and with the aid of angels.

## Angels as protectors and rescuers

God's angels minister to His people in times of need and danger. There have been many times in history that God has used angels to come to the aid of His children. God used angels to guide the children of Israel through the wilderness and into the Promised Land (Exodus 23:20-23). It was an angel of the Lord who stood between the children of Israel and the Egyptian army until they could cross the Red Sea (Exodus 14:19f). Elijah was fed by angels as he was fleeing in the desert (1 Kings 19:5). A company of angels saved Elisha and his servant from the Syrian army (2 Kings 6:14). An angel of the Lord killed 185,000 in the Assyrian army to protect Jerusalem (2 Kings 19:35).

In the New Testament, God continued to send His angels to rescue and protect His people. After the death of Christ on the cross, and after the experience in the Upper Room at Pentecost, Peter was thrown into prison. The possibility of escape from that prison seemed remote. In Acts 12:6 we read that,

> Peter was sleeping between two soldiers, bound with two chains; and guards in front of the door were watching the prison.

The situation looked hopeless for Peter. But God is the God of hopeless situations, and Peter was rescued by an angel of the Lord. After his experience with the angel, he said,

> Now I know for sure that the Lord has sent forth His angel and rescued me from the hand of Herod and from all that the Jewish people were expecting.
>
> Acts 12:11

## THE ANGELIC SPIRIT WORLD

In Billy Graham's book, *Angels: God's Secret Agents*, there are many stories about how God has sent His angels to rescue or protect. And there are many Christians who can recall stories of how they were miraculously rescued from disaster. Perhaps God sent angels in many of these situations.

One such story was revealed in an interview with the wife of a veteran American missionary in Luzon.

> There were five women in the car as we were driving for two hours to Manila for a conference for Christian women. As we were driving down a hill, a man stepped right out in front of us and we hit him with the car. He was thrown a great distance and killed. All five of us got out of the car to see what we could do. As we did, a hostile crowd began to form. Then a Filipino drove up and immediately told us to get back into the car and follow him. We did as he said, and followed him through a series of one-way streets and backstreets until we arrived at a police station. He stayed with us helping to translate to the policeman who took our report. When we were finished we thanked him and asked for his address. He gave us an address but when we later went to that address it did not exist. No one in the area had even heard of the man. I think that the man must have been an angel sent to help and protect us.

Sceptics will be quick to point out that there could be other explanations for the story above. But angelic explanations should not be surprising to students of the Bible. God has said in the Bible that there is angelic protection for His people.

> For He will give His angels charge concerning you, to guard you in all your ways. They will bear you up in their hands.
>
> Psalm 91:11,12

> The angel of the Lord encamps around those who fear Him, and rescues them.
>
> Psalm 34:7

It has been shown from the Bible that God has sent His angels to protect and rescue His people. We see from the previous texts that God intends to use angels to continue to rescue His people today. Angels are as real today as they were in Bible times.

> But Scripture strongly insists upon teaching us what could most effectively make for our consolation and the strengthening of our faith: namely, that angels are dispensers and administrators of God's beneficence toward us. For this reason, Scripture recalls that they keep vigil for our safety, take upon themselves our defense, direct our ways, and take care that some harm may not befall us (Calvin 1977:166).

## Angels as spectators

God knows every detail of our lives. He is omniscient. He knows our innermost feelings and the number of hairs on our heads. God also has angels to watch us. Paul expresses this idea in 1 Corinthians 4:9,

> ... We have become a spectacle to the world, both to angels and to men.

Besides having a God who knows us, we have angels who know us and are familiar with us.

As this book begins its discussion of the evil realm of the spirit world, it should be comforting for God's people to realize that God has angels at His disposal for man's protection and help.

These angels constitute a vast spirit world army who were created by God to do His will on behalf of man. This spirit world army of God is on the side of His people so that they can do battle against the forces of the Evil One.

# 5
# FROM LUCIFER TO SATAN

It was a wonderful spirit world which God created — a "world" of perfection and beauty. However, one of those beautiful angelic beings led a rebellion in heaven which would drastically change the universe. The leader of this angelic revolution was Lucifer, who then became Satan.

Scripture does not lay out for the reader a systematic theology of Satan. It is necessary to develop this theology by seeing Satan interact with both God and man in Scripture. It is important in this study of Satan to distinguish between reputation and reality. Satan's reputation is what people think or perceive him to be. This is surrounded by a great deal of tradition. The following is an attempt at discovering the reality of Satan from Scripture.

## SATAN'S ORIGINAL STATE

Very little is told the reader of Scripture about the origins of Satan. He enters the Bible drama at the beginning of human history in the Garden of Eden. Without introduction, he appears as a serpent in all his evil and deceitful glory to tempt Adam and Eve into rebellion against God.

> Satan appears in Scripture as the recognized head of the fallen angels. He was originally, it would seem, one of the mightiest princes of the angelic world, and became the leader of those that revolted and fell away from God (Berkhof 1939:148).

The Bible suggests that Satan was not created in the evil state in which he is seen in Scripture and experienced by man. Ezekiel 28:12-15 describes Satan in terms of the King of Tyre. This description paints a picture of a being of great majesty and beauty who lives in the presence of God. The clue that this passage is referring to Satan, as well as the king of Tyre, is in the statement "You were in Eden, the garden of God."

> ... You had the seal of perfection,
> Full of wisdom and perfect in beauty.
> You were in Eden, the garden of God;
> Every precious stone was your covering:
> The ruby, the topaz, and the diamond;
> The beryl, the onyx, and the jasper;
> The lapis lazuli, the turquoise, and the emerald;
> And the gold, the workmanship of your settings and sockets,
> Was in you.
> On the day that you were created
> They were prepared.
> You were the anointed cherub who covers,
> And I placed you there.
> You were on the holy mountain of God;
> You walked in the midst of the stones of fire.
> You were blameless in your ways
> From the day you were created,
> Until unrighteousness was found in you.

Satan was a part of God's creation which He declared to be "very good" (Genesis 1:31). God created Satan, as He also created man — in perfection and beauty. The beauty of Satan is described in this text in terms of his being covered with jewels and gold. He was created "perfect in beauty." In Isaiah 14:12, he is called "the star of the morning" or Lucifer (King James Version). As Lucifer, his beauty was such that he shone as if he were a star which could be seen in the bright sky of the morning. This is certainly a different description than the Satan of tradition with horns and pointed tail.

Here, Satan is called "the anointed cherub," therefore, he is an angel. The fact that he was "anointed" suggests that he was given a position of honor in heaven by God. He was placed on the "holy mountain of God" and "walked in the midst of the stones of fire." Heaven was his home and he walked in the midst of the heavenly host of angelic spirit beings.

God created him "full of wisdom." It is certainly no surprise that an "anointed cherub" would have great wisdom. Satan's wisdom would certainly extend to the things of God. He lived in the very presence of God, Satan knows about God from first-hand experience.

God said that He created Satan "blameless" and that he "had the seal of perfection." It is certainly difficult to understand how a being who was created perfect could degenerate to the point of becoming the author of all evil. But this was the case. Though created in perfection, he was also created with the variable factor of choice. Satan's evil and deceitful nature was not because of God's creation, but the result of his own perversion. Satan became evil by choice.

> Yet, since the devil was created by God, let us remember that this malice, which we attribute to his nature, came not from his creation but from his perversion. For, whatever he has that is to be condemned he has derived from his revolt and fall (Calvin 1977:175).

## Satan's Pride and Subsequent Fall

Ezekiel 28:12-15 describes Lucifer as the beautiful star of the morning who was created in perfection, wisdom, and beauty. The end of verse 15 shows an abrupt change in Lucifer's situation.

> You were blameless in your ways
> From the day you were created,
> Until unrighteousness was found in you.
> By the abundance of your trade
> You were internally filled with violence,
> And you sinned;
> Therefore I have cast you as profane
> From the mountain of God
> And I have destroyed you, O covering cherub,
> From the midst of the stones of fire.
> Your heart was lifted up because of your beauty;
> You corrupted your wisdom by reason of your splendor.
> I cast you to the ground.
>
> Ezekiel 28:15-17

Satan's beauty became his downfall; its resultant splendor warped and corrupted his wisdom. Isaiah 14:12-15 gives more help in understanding the corruption and rebellion of Satan.

> How you have fallen from heaven,
> O star of the morning, son of the dawn!
> You have been cut down to the earth,
> You who have weakened the nations!
> But you said in your heart;
> "I will ascend to heaven;
> I will raise my throne above the stars of God,
> And I will sit on the mount of assembly
> In the recesses of the north.

> I will ascend above the heights of the clouds;
> I will make myself like the Most High."

This passage gives insight into what is meant by the words "your heart was lifted up because of your beauty." Satan's heart was "lifted up" when he said the five "I will's." The five "I will's" of this text are summarized in the final "I will make myself like the Most High." Satan's beauty caused such intense pride that he was not satisfied with his position of honor among the heavenly host. His pride in his beauty and splendor caused him to desire a more exalted position and even equality with God. This was his sin.

Satan's sin of pride caused God to cast him to earth, because the holiness of God cannot be contaminated by sin.

> Therefore I have cast you as profane from the mountain of God.
> Ezekiel 28:16

Satan would no longer be a heavenly being. He would no longer be Lucifer, the star of the morning, but he would be Satan, the adversary (Strong 1907:454).

## SATAN'S DOMAIN

From Isaiah and Ezekiel, it is seen that Satan was cast out of heaven and sent to the earth.

> You have been cut down to the earth.
> Isaiah 14:12

> I cast you to the ground.
> Ezekiel 28:17

The earth would be Satan's domain, making him a *this worldly* spirit being.

There is further evidence of this in the names given to Satan in the New Testament. The Bible calls him both the "god of this world" (2 Corinthians 4:4) and the "prince of this world" (John 12:31). Satan is also called the "prince of the power of the air," indicating that his domain extends into the atmosphere.

Satan himself tells of his domain when questioned by God, as narrated in Job 1:6-7.

> Now there was a day when the sons of God came to present themselves before the LORD, Satan also came among them. And the LORD said to Satan, "From where do you come?" Then Satan answered the Lord and said, "From roaming about on the earth and walking around on it."

Though Satan's domain as a *this worldly* spirit being is the earth, it appears from the above text that he also has access to heaven.

## SATAN'S RELATIONSHIP TO GOD AND MAN

Satan is "the adversary." As such, he is the enemy or opponent of both God and man.

> The word "Satan" means "adversary" — primarily to God, secondarily to men; the term "devil" signifies "slanderer" — of God to men, and of men to God. It is indicated also in the description of the "man of sin" as "he that opposeth and exalteth himself against all that is called God."
> (Strong 1907:454).

Satan never ceases to try to make himself equal with God. It is this ambition of Satan which puts him at odds with God who commands, "Thou shalt have no other gods besides Me." God and Satan are at cross-purposes.

On earth Satan would have to live under the authority of man. When man was created, God said to him, "rule... over all the earth" (Genesis 1:26). The Psalmist says that,

> The heavens are the heavens of the Lord; but the earth
> He has given to the sons of men.
> Psalm 115:16

It was God's plan that the perfect man and woman He created should exercise authority over Satan. At that time the man and the woman enjoyed a perfect relationship with God. Satan had violated his relationship with God in trying to be His equal and was cast to earth to live under man's authority.

The story of man giving up his authority of the earth to Satan is told in Genesis 3. Here, Satan appears to man in the form of a serpent. It appears from this text that Satan has no authority to force the man and the woman to do anything. He simply tempts man with the same element that caused his own fall, the temptation to be like God.

> Now the serpent was more crafty than any beast of the field which the LORD God had made. And he said to the woman, "Indeed, has God said, 'You shall not eat from any tree of the garden'?" And the woman said to the serpent, "From the fruit of the trees of the garden we may eat, but from the fruit of the tree which is in the middle of the garden, God has said, 'You shall not eat from it or touch it, lest you die.'" And the serpent said to the woman, "You surely shall not die! For God knows that in the day you eat from it your eyes will be opened, and you will be like God, knowing good and evil."
> Genesis 3:1–5

The key element of Satan's temptation is in the words "and you will be like God" (Genesis 3:5). Compare this to Satan's words in Isaiah 14:14, "I will make myself like the Most High."

Satan knew that man was the object of God's love. It is his desire to attack God by attacking the object of God's love, man. He knows that if man could be enticed to sin then the God/man relationship would be broken as his relationship with God had been.

> The special sin of these angels is not revealed, but has generally been thought to consist in this; that they exalted themselves over against God, and aspired to supreme authority. If this ambition played an important part in the life of Satan and led to his downfall, it would at once explain why he tempted man on the particular point and sought to lure him to his destruction by appealing to a possible similar ambition in man (Berkhof 1941:148).

Man was created to live under the authority of God and, in turn, to exercise authority over "all the earth" which included Satan. Satan was tempting man to reject the authority of God, and instead "be like God" or equal to Him. The man and the woman chose to believe the lies of Satan resulting in sin and separation from God. The consequence of man's sin was separation from God. This separation caused man to forfeit his authority over the earth and Satan. Subsequently, Satan became the god and prince of this world (2 Corinthians 4:4). 1 John 5:19 declares that,

> ... the whole world lies in the power of the evil one.

## SATAN'S WORK

Because Satan is not omnipresent, his work is often carried out for him by angels who are loyal to him — angels who were also cast out of heaven by God. So it is often difficult to differentiate between Satan's personal work and that of his loyal angels. But Satan is ultimately responsible for his angels because they carry out his will, just as God's angels reflect and carry out His perfect will and plan.

> He (Satan) controls many subordinate evil spirits; there is only one devil, but there are many angels or demons, and through their agency Satan may accomplish his purposes (Strong 1907:455).

Paul states that man's real enemy is Satan and his many angels.

> For our struggle is not against flesh and blood, but against the rulers, against the powers, against the world forces of this darkness, against the spiritual forces of wickedness in the heavenly places.
>
> Ephesians 6:12

The whole context of this passage in Ephesians tells of battle and warfare. Satan and his army of fallen angels are at odds with God and His people. Satan is attacking God's people to get even with God. The war is between God and Satan, but God's people have been brought into the fighting because of Satan's attacks. Satan, the adversary, is the opponent of both God and man.

Satan's single goal is to keep man away from a faith relationship with God. It was suggested in Chapter 3 that all men are separated from God because of their sin and God's holiness. The way to restore the relationship between God and man is through forgiveness by faith in the death of Jesus. Faith is the key element for man's salvation. It is here that Satan is the most active, attacking man on the issue of faith in God. If Satan can prevent faith in the heart of an unbeliever or destroy faith in a believer, then his purpose is accomplished.

Paul describes the work of Satan in the minds of unbelievers in terms of his causing a blindness to the gospel:

> And even if our gospel is veiled, it is veiled to those who are perishing, in whose case the god of this world has blinded the minds of the unbelieving, that they might

not see the light of the gospel of the glory of Christ, who is the image of God.

2 Corinthians 4:3–4

Jesus also tells of this work of the Devil in His parable of the sower. In this parable, Jesus is teaching the various ways in which the gospel message is received by man. The first description tells of Satan stealing the message from the minds of the unbelievers hearing the word, or message of salvation in Christ.

> And these are the ones who are beside the road where the word is sown; and when they hear, immediately Satan comes and takes away the word which has been sown in them.
>
> Mark 4:15

By keeping the unbeliever away from a faith relationship with God, Satan keeps him under his authority as the god and prince of this world. Satan's attack on the unbeliever is simply to convince him that sin is not so bad. God's Word says that sin will eternally separate God and man. Satan counters this with "how could something (sin) which is so enjoyable and feels so right be against God's will?" The issue for the unbeliever becomes whom to believe, God or Satan.

Dr. George Ladd, in his book *The Gospel of the Kingdom*, clearly states Satan's primary goal regarding man:

> How often we fail to understand satanic devices! A man may be a cultured, ethical and even religious person and yet be in demonic darkness. Satan's basic desire is to keep men from Christ. His primary concern is not to corrupt morals nor to make atheists nor to produce enemies of religion (Ladd 1959:31).

Satan's attack on the believer or child of God is also on this element of faith. He does everything he can to cause the believer to doubt God and the sufficiency of Christ's death on the cross. By so doing he hopes to weaken or destroy the believer's faith relationship with God through Christ. Paul expresses this when he says to the Corinthian church:

> But I am afraid, lest as the serpent deceived Eve by his craftiness, your minds should be led astray from the simplicity and purity of devotion to Christ.
> 2 Corinthians 11:3

This attack on the faith of the believer also comes in Satan's role as the accuser of God's people:

> ...Now the salvation, and the power, and the kingdom of our God and the authority of His Christ have come, for the accuser of our brethren has been thrown down, who accuses them before our God day and night. And they overcame him because of the blood of the Lamb and because of the word of their testimony, and they did not love their life even to death.
> Revelation 12:10,11

Satan is the accuser of God's people. He is constantly bringing charges against them. The charge that Satan brings against the believer is that he is a sinner who is unworthy to be a child of the Most High God. Satan attacks the believer to make him think that he is worthy only of God's condemnation and not His salvation. He tries to get the believer to look within himself to find righteousness which would make him worthy to have a relationship with God. Satan, through his accusations, attempts to attack the believer by shifting the ground of salvation from faith in Christ to personal worthiness.

The Bible calls Satan "the father of lies" (John 8:44) and the "deceiver" (Revelation 20:10). As the father of lies and the great deceiver, Satan will stop at nothing to convince the believer and the unbeliever that they do not need God. He can be as subtle or as bold as the situation requires. He is indeed a powerful and "crafty" (Genesis 3:1) spirit being who is bent on man's destruction.

This warning of the Apostle Peter summarizes Satan's desire to destroy man:

> Be of sober spirit, be on the alert. Your adversary, the devil, prowls about like a roaring lion, seeking someone to devour.
>
> 1 Peter 5:8

In *The Presence of the Future*, Dr. George Ladd pinpoints the object of Satan's attacks:

> Satan is the enemy of God's kingdom and does all he can to frustrate its work among men (Matthew 13:19,39). However, we do not discover the idea of Satan attacking the Kingdom of God or exercising his power against the Kingdom itself. He can only wage his war against the sons of the Kingdom (Ladd 1974:161).

Satan was created as a beautiful, anointed cherub who enjoyed the presence of God and the hosts of heaven. He is familiar with God and His ways. As the great deceiver and liar he can use this knowledge of God for his own evil purposes. Nowhere does Scripture suggest that Satan was stripped of his power and beauty which was part of his original creation. He is still the powerful and beautiful spirit being who is the leader of an army of evil angels bent on the destruction of God's people.

Satan's primary target is man's faith relationship with God. As such, his focus is on the ultimate concerns. However, he uses his *this worldly* army of demons in matters of everyday concerns to distract and lure man away from God.

# 6
# THE DEMONIC SPIRIT WORLD

Satan attempts to challenge God and His angels in every way possible. This normally takes place on earth — the domain of Satan. But since Satan is not omnipresent, he has a host of loyal spirit world beings who carry out his evil will.

## DEMONS ARE FALLEN ANGELS

The Bible uses the term "demon" to refer to those angels who are loyal to Satan. Matthew 25:41 speaks of demons when it refers to "the Devil and his angels." It is nearly impossible to separate the nature and work of demons from the nature and work of their leader, Satan. Their history as *other worldly* spirit beings is inseparably linked to that of Satan. And because of their loyalty to him, so is their history as *this worldly* spirit beings.

On the sixth day of God's creation story we are told that "God saw all that He had made, and behold, it was very good" (Genesis 1:31). This was a time in history in which every element of creation was perfect, and working together in harmony under the authority and dominion of God. God enjoyed an intimate relationship with man. To man, He gave the rule over all the earth and everything in it (Genesis 1:26). In the spirit world all was in harmony with God because everything was "very good." Even Lucifer, who later became Satan, was created "perfect in beauty" and "blameless" (Ezekiel 28:12,15). However, the perfection of God's creation did not last. Because of the sin of pride, God cast Lucifer to earth. Scripture continues this story of rebellion in the heavenly places by showing that Lucifer was not alone in his rebellion against God:

> God did not spare angels when they sinned, but cast them into hell and committed them to pits of darkness, reserved for judgment.
>
> 2 Peter 2:4

> And angels who did not keep their own domain, but abandoned their proper abode, He has kept in eternal bonds under darkness for the judgment of the great day.
>
> Jude 6

These texts do not specifically mention the sin for which these angels were cast out of heaven. But since the fall of Lucifer and the fall of man was the result of the pride of exalting themselves to equality with God, it would seem probable that this was also the sin of the angels.

There is one text that seems to link the fall of Satan with that of the rebellious angels:

> And the great dragon was thrown down, the serpent of old who is called the Devil and Satan, who deceives the whole world; he was thrown down to the earth and his angels were thrown down with him.
>
> Revelation 12:9

This sin and fall from heaven brought a drastic change in the character of these fallen angels. While once they surrounded the throne of God giving Him honor and glory, now they seek to destroy everything dear to God. As angels they desired to be obedient to God. As demons they are the enemies of God who are obedient to Satan, the adversary; as *this worldly* spirit beings, these demons aid Satan in his task of keeping man from relationship with God.

Demons are not ignorant of God, His will, or His power. As angels they enjoyed an existence as *other worldly* spirit beings who stood in the presence of God Himself. They know about God from firsthand experience.

> You believe that God is one. You do well; the demons also believe, and shudder.
>
> James 2:19

It is this knowledge about God that makes them powerful in their dealings with man, because they are able to mix their lies with enough truth to make the deception attractive.

Demons are not ignorant about Jesus Christ. In the gospel of Mark, demons address Jesus as "the Holy One of God" (Mark 1:24), "the Son of God" (Mark 3:11) or "the Son of the Most High God" (Mark 5:7).

> That the demonic powers possess a certain knowledge of Jesus' identity is clear from the cry of recognition, "I know who you are, the Holy One of God." The unclean spirit recognizes Jesus as the Holy One of God (Lane 1974:73).

## DEMONS CONSTITUTE AN ENORMOUS ARMY

Scripture does not tell of the organization or number of demons. However, the Bible does give a hint as to the multitude of these fallen angels. It was already observed from Revelation 5:11 that there are millions and millions of angels surrounding the throne of God. Another passage, in Revelation 12:4 tells of the dragon (Satan) bringing down one-third of the angels to earth. "And his tail swept away a third of the stars of heaven, and threw them to the earth." Even with only one-third of the angels becoming demons, their number is still in millions.

This should not be surprising to students of the New Testament. Mark 16:9 says that Mary Magdalene had seven demons cast out of her by Jesus. In an account in Mark 5:1-15, there is indication that a "legion" (3,000 to 6,000) of demons possessed a Gerasene man. When these demons were cast out, they went into 2,000 swine. Suffice it to say, that the demonic army is enormous.

## VARIETY IN THE DEMONIC SPIRIT WORLD

As is the case with the seraphim and cherubim of the angelic spirit world, there is variety in the demonic spirit world. It is impossible to tell from Scripture whether the difference is in their individual make-up, as with seraphim and cherubim, or merely in their functions. In some cases the Scripture gives no description of these demonic spirits but simply gives their name. It is then necessary to go to history for descriptions of these spirit beings.

The prophet Isaiah makes mention of a strange spirit which was supposed to live in the ruins of Babylon after the judgment of God. In the *King James Version* (KJV), this spirit being is translated as a "satyr" (Isaiah 13:21 and 34:14). A satyr is a creature which has the head and body of a man and the legs of a goat. The *New American Standard Bible* (NASB) chose to translate that word as "shaggy goats" and "hairy goats." However, there are marginal notes in both places which identify them as "goat demons" and "demon," respectively.

These goat demons were, apparently important spirit world beings to Israel because the people were being tempted to worship and sacrifice to these demons and their idols. That this was displeasing to God is obvious in Leviticus 17:7 (NASB),

> And they shall no longer sacrifice their sacrifices to the goat demons with which they play the harlot. This shall be a permanent statute to them throughout their generations.

The passage in Isaiah 34:14 mentions another spirit being who will inhabit the ruins of Babylon. "Yes, the night monster shall settle there" (NASB). "Night monster" is a translation of the word "Lilith." Lilith was well known in Assyria as a female demon who lived in desolate places (Montgomery 1976:33).

John Calvin comments on this text of Isaiah 34:14 which mentions both the "satyr" and the "night monster."

> Though we cannot absolutely determine whether the Prophet means witches, or goblins, or satyrs and fauns, yet it is universally agreed that these words denote animals which have the shape of men. We see also what various delusions are practiced by Satan, what phantoms and hideous monsters are seen, and what sounds and noises are heard (Calvin: volume 3, p.56).

In the Revelation of John concerning God's wrath and judgment, John sees a vision of unclean spirits or demons which are like frogs.

> And I saw coming out of the mouth of the dragon and out of the mouth of the beast and out of the mouth of the false prophet, three unclean spirits like frogs; for they are spirits of demons, performing signs...
> Revelation 16:13-14

It was seen in the previous chapter that there is variety in the angelic spirit world. From the above texts it is also apparent that there is also variety in the demonic spirit world. But this should follow from the fact that the demonic spirit world is the angelic spirit world fallen and cast down to earth.

## SPECIALIZATION IN THE DEMONIC SPIRIT WORLD

There are a few different names given to demons in the Bible which give certain suggestions as to their function or specialization in the *this worldly* spirit world. The Bible is not clear whether these names suggest something about the nature of certain demons or simply something about the function which is being performed at that time in the life of that particular person.

## Demons and the dead

In the Old Testament, the term "familiar spirit" is often used to refer to demons. Mediums, those who supposedly communicate with the dead, are said to be possessed of a familiar spirit. As *this worldly* spirit beings, these demonic familiar spirits are intimately knowledgeable of the affairs of man. Like angels, these spirits are spectators of people's lives. Familiar spirits are "familiar" with the lives of men and women.

It is possible that a medium is not really contacting the dead but merely calling on a demon who is familiar with the life of the dead person. As such, the familiar spirit would know intimate details of the dead person's life and could even attempt to imitate his voice.

## Demons and divination

Divination is the practice of giving information, usually about the future, which is not available by natural means. This information is given to the diviner by higher powers. These higher powers are variously described as psychic, a special ability in the mind of the diviner; or as spiritual, a communication to the diviner from the spirit world. The diviner "reads" this information from these higher powers with the use of a variety of objects: tarot cards, a crystal ball, the palm of the hand, the liver of an animal, tea leaves at the bottom of a cup, oil added to water, astrology, or a ouija board.

This information from the diviner is provided — usually sold — to his client to enable him to know what to do about the future. The client of a diviner seeks this special information because he is anxious about the future. He believes that too many of life's decisions are left to chance or luck. By having this information about the future, the anxiety of the client is reduced and he is better able to make decisions.

The New Testament provides one interesting case of a female diviner. This will be used as a case study to see what light can be shed on divination from a New Testament perspective, which relates divination to the demonic spirit world.

> And it happened that as we were going to the place of prayer, a certain slave-girl having a spirit of divination met us, who was bringing her masters much profit by fortune-telling. Following after Paul and us, she kept crying out saying, "These men are good servants of the Most High God, who are proclaiming to you the way of salvation." And she continued doing this for many days. But Paul was greatly annoyed, and turned and said to the spirit, "I command you in the name of Jesus Christ to come out of her!" And it came out at that very moment. But when her masters saw that their hope of profit was gone, they seized Paul and Silas and dragged them into the market place before the authorities.
>
> Acts 16:16–19

The case of the female diviner presents several characteristics of divination.

**1. Divination is not a special ability, but the work of a spirit.** The fortune-telling ability of the girl is said to have come from a "spirit of divination." The Apostle Paul separates the person of the girl from that of the spirit when he addresses the spirit directly in casting it out. If her power to divine the future were an ability, Paul would have dealt with the girl directly.

**2. Divination is not necessarily a trick or a fraud.** Both historically and presently, the profession of divination has had plenty of frauds whose only desire was to trick people for money. But this was not the case with this slave-girl. First, the text identifies the spirit as a "spirit of divination." Apparently, the spirit manifested itself through the girl by giving her the power to tell the future. Second, the Apostle Paul would not have dealt with the spirit if the divination were a mere fraud. He would have exhorted or scolded the slave-girl and her owners for cheating people of their money and would not have cast out the spirit. Finally, if the divination were a fraud, the owners of the slave-girl would not have been so upset with Paul for casting out the spirit. Even without the spirit, a fraud could continue to bring them profit.

**3. Divination was dealt with like demon possession.** As with the case of the Gerasene demoniac, the spirit is spoken to directly. The command in both cases is simply "come out." The authority backing up the command of the Apostle Paul is in the fact that he is doing this "in the name of Jesus." This is the same way in which demons are dealt with repeatedly in Scripture.

**4. The diviner had the external appearances of Christianity.** In her actions and her words, she could easily have been identified as a Christian. The text says that she was a follower of the Apostle Paul "for many days." She kept crying out, "These men are bond-servants of the Most High God, who are proclaiming to you the way of salvation." This slave-girl was certainly right about the men being servants of God. This would certainly not anger Paul. She also proclaimed that these men were preaching "the way of salvation." It would appear that she believed Paul's message and was endorsing this message to others. Paul should have been pleased at this girl but he was "greatly annoyed." Paul was annoyed with the spirit, not the words of the girl, and cast the spirit out. He was not fooled by the external trappings of the diviner's Christian words and actions. He knew that he was dealing with a demon, and therefore cast it out.

**5. Why would this young diviner be so interested in following Paul and identifying herself with Paul's message of salvation?** By doing this, she was giving her "gift" and occupation Christian credibility. We see this so often here in the Philippines. Those who are fortune-tellers and diviners identify themselves with the Christian church and the Christian message so that it appears that their "gift" comes from God. But, indeed, such identification with the people and message of God does not ensure that the power to divine the future comes from God. With the slave-girl, we see her identification with the people and message of God, and yet, her power for divination came from a demon spirit.

## Demons and sickness

There are several New Testament texts which indicate that some sickness is caused by the spirit world. In the Gospel of Mark, Jesus addresses the demonic spirit as "you deaf and dumb spirit." Apparently, the destructive nature of this demon had kept this boy from hearing and speaking.

> And when Jesus saw that a crowd was rapidly gathering, He rebuked the unclean spirit, saying to it, "You deaf and

> dumb spirit, I command you, come out of him and do not enter him again."
>
> Mark 9:25

In Matthew, it was a demon who caused a man to be both blind and mute.

> Then there was brought to Him a demon-possessed man who was blind and dumb, and He healed him, so that the dumb man spoke and saw.
>
> Matthew 12:22

That spirits can cause sickness is also clear from the following account.

> And He was teaching in one of the synagogues on the Sabbath. And behold, there was a woman who for eighteen years had had a sickness caused by a spirit; and she was bent double, and could not straighten up at all. And when Jesus saw her, He called her over and said to her, "Woman, you are freed from your sickness."
>
> Luke 13:10–12

On another occasion demon possession was closely tied to what appeared to be epilepsy. In Matthew 17:14-20, a father brings his son to Jesus claiming that the son has epilepsy. Instead of dealing with this as a sickness Jesus cast out the demon and the boy was healed "at once." Though Jesus often healed sickness, in this case He recognized that the boy's problem had all the symptoms of a physical illness but was in reality caused by the demonic spirit world.

There is a variety in the demonic spirit world of fallen angels both in their descriptions and their strategies.

> God created angels, spirits intended to implement His general and redemptive purposes in the world (Hebrews 1:14). One of the highest of these created, angelic spirits rebelled against God and by his own will (and more ultimate cause) became the devil. Others who were filled with pride and wanted to become as God joined Satan in his rebellion. These fallen angels are called spirits or demons. Since their fall, there has been a great battle among the unseen powers of good and evil. Teaching on the reality of the kingdom of darkness, as well as the kingdom of God permeates the Scriptures from beginning to end (Lewis in Montgomery 1976:353).

These hostile spiritual beings have the potential power of possession, obsession, influence and temptation. It is important for the believer to know this enemy and his tactics in order to be able to "stand firm" and "resist the devil."

Satan can also affect the lives of people through the practitioners of his power. These practitioners use Satan's power to meet the everyday concerns of sickness (physical and spirit-caused) and uncertainty about the future. The believer and the church must be equipped to discern the source of power of those who are spirit world practitioners.

# 7
# DEMONIZATION

The subject of demonization or demon possession is a point at which the spirit worldview of the Bible comes into great conflict with the scientific worldview. This conflict of worldviews involves the disciplines of theology, medicine and psychology. A.R. Tippet suggests that to understand demonization, it will be necessary for the researcher to identify with the spirit worldview on this subject.

> One reason why western theologians, medical men and psychologists have trouble with the cross-cultural study of demon possession is that they refuse to do their thinking outside their own scientific worldview (Tippet in Montgomery 1976:144).

W. Stanley Mooneyhan, former President of World Vision International, supports the need for a worldview shift in understanding or seeing demonic activity. This shift for perceiving the spirit world is necessary for a westerner but not for a Filipino who already has a spirit worldview.

> I am sure that had I had a different cultural background and different "eyes" for perceiving the world, I might have seen the visible manifestations of this demonic activity.

> My technology-oriented, rationalistic, western culture simply prevented me from seeing what the people of other cultures see and experience in a more tangible way (Mooneyhan in Montgomery 1976:215).

## DEMONIZATION FROM A SPIRIT WORLD PERSPECTIVE

Nowhere is the conflict between the Filipino spirit worldview and the scientific worldview more apparent than in the area of demonization.

From a spirit worldview, demon possession is the phenomenon whereby a person is indwelt with one or more demons. This indwelling demon is then able to take control of the body or mind, or both, of the person being possessed. The possessed person carries out the will of the demon while under its control, and can even manifest the character and voice of the demon or demons. Demon possession is an explanation system for a radical change in a person's behavior pattern, based on the person being acted upon by the external forces of demons.

> Reviewing the series of cases which have just been cited, their first and most striking characteristic is that the patient's organism appears to be invaded by a new personality; it is governed by a strange soul. This is what has given to these states, from the earliest times when we can observe them up to the most recent, the name of "possession." It is as if another soul had entered into the body and henceforward subsisted there, in place of or side by side with the normal subject (Oesterreich 1966:17).

Dr. Basil Jackson, Chairman of the Department of Psychiatry, Lutheran Hospital of Milwaukee, Wisconsin, emphasizes the element of demonic control of the human will and body as another evidence of demonic possession.

> One of the chief characteristics of demonization is the possession of the will of the individual with resulting control over his body. If we are to believe many of the records, it appears that, in those instances where the possessing spirit was prepared to speak, it not only often spoke with a different voice, but it spoke of itself as an entity separate from the possessed individual (Jackson in Montgomery 1976:265).

Further symptoms of demonic possession or attacks are given by John Richards in his book, *But Deliver Us From Evil: An Introduction to the Demonic Dimension in Pastoral Care* (1974:156).

**A. Change in personality** including intelligence, moral character, demeanor, appearance

**B. Physical changes**
  1. Preternatural strength
  2. Epileptic convulsions; foaming
  3. Catatonic symptoms, falling
  4. Clouding of consciousness, anesthesia to pain
  5. Changed voice

**C. Mental changes**
  1. Glossolalia; understanding unknown languages
  2. Preternatural knowledge
  3. Psychic and occult powers, e.g., clairvoyance, telepathy and prediction

**D. Spiritual changes**
  1. Reaction to and fear of Christ; blasphemy with regret as in depression

2. Affected by prayer
From the list of possible symptoms for demon possession, it is clear that demons can control and, therefore, change any part of the human body or mind.

## DEMONIZATION FROM A SCIENTIFIC PERSPECTIVE

The scientific explanation for this same phenomenon comes under the disciplines of psychology and psychiatry. Virtually all of the symptoms mentioned above regarding demon possession could also have naturalistic (physical or emotional) causes and explanations.

> The symptoms mentioned in the Bible, or added by latter observers, can almost all be explained in some naturalistic way. Of course this does not rule out possession as the cause of these behaviors, but it shows that what people call demonic today, may not be demonic at all. Drugs, loss of sleep, psychosis, epileptic seizures, transcendental meditation, physical disease, intense fear — these are among the factors which can lead to symptoms that apparently are identical to the cited signs of demon possession.

> One other psychological observation must be mentioned at this point. There is abundant evidence from studies in perceptual psychology that people see and act in accordance with the expectation of those around them. If someone convinces me I am demon possessed, unconsciously I might begin to experience the symptoms and show the behavior which fit the diagnosis (Montgomery 1976:245).

A scientific explanation of a person who displays a radical change in personality and behavior so that he seems to have two or more personalities is called "schizophrenia." A schizophrenic suffers from delusions and can hear voices speaking to him. This type of thought and behavior is explained by psychology in terms of competing personalities within the person with each personality manifesting itself at different times and under different circumstances (Mezer 1970:74).

The manifestation of radical personality changes with its resultant bizarre behavior has two separate explanations depending on the worldview. Besides the scientific worldview explanation, the spirit worldview explains it in terms of the external forces of demons taking control of the person and causing him to display, at times, the personality of the demon. Science says that such a person does not hear voices; he hears only his disturbed mind. The other worldview says that the person hears voices because there are really demons speaking to them.

It is beyond the scope of this book to resolve the conflict of what appears to be two competing worldviews. The validity of the scientific explanation of mental illness cannot be denied. However, the spirit worldview tells of another explanation of bizarre personality changes and behavior which is caused by the *this worldly* spirit world of demons. The Bible comes down on the side of the spirit world explanation system. However this biblical explanation need not compete as an alternative to the scientific explanation but should be put alongside it as another possible cause of the same phenomenon.

## DISCERNMENT OF PSYCHOLOGICAL, PHYSICAL AND DEMONIC CAUSES

In the Bible, demon possession finds its focal point in the gospels of Matthew, Mark and Luke. In these records of the life of Christ on earth, it is quite obvious that Jesus' dealings with demons made up a very significant part of His ministry. He was met with a constant stream of persons who were demon possessed, and on each occasion He cast out the demon or demons.

It is apparent from the life and words of Jesus that He differentiated between illness (physical sickness) and demon possession. Many times in the gospels, Jesus talks about healing the sick *and* casting out demons.

> And his fame went throughout all Syria: and they brought unto him all sick people that were taken with diverse (various) diseases and torments, and those which were possessed with devils (demons), and those which were lunatick (mentally ill), and those that had the palsy (paralysis); and he healed them.
> Matthew 4:24 *KJV*
> (phrases within parentheses supplied by the author)

> And having summoned His twelve disciples, He gave them authority over unclean spirits, to cast them out, and to heal every kind of disease and every kind of sickness.
> Matthew 10:1

Jesus had no difficulty explaining some bizarre behavior as a medical problem and at other times as problems from the spirit world. Medical explanations need not compete and be exclusive of spirit world explanations. Rather, each can be a valid explanation of phenomena which have similar manifestations.

There was no discussion in the Bible as to whether the person's problem or symptom came from physical, emotional or demonic cause. Jesus and his disciples just seemed to know.

> The difficulty lies in the fact that in none of the Bible's teaching is there a discussion as to how one determines when a demon is present. Are the few descriptions in the Gospels and Acts typical of all cases? Even if they are, the details are meager and case histories almost non-existent (White in Montgomery 1976:285).

Dr. John White, former Professor of Psychiatry at the University of Manitoba, Canada, gives some helpful hints for developing the "clinical picture" of those who may be victims of demonic activity.

### The History

The history is sometimes one of contact with magic or the occult either innocently (i.e., with no deliberate defiance of God in mind) or in chosen rebellion. Anything from Satanism to teacup reading may be implicated. There is strong evidence that real demonic manifestations can follow such contracts.

### Signs and Symptoms Specific to Demonic Influence

These consist of a virulent hostile or fearful reaction to the things of God, so that the mention of His name, the name of Jesus, or specific references to the redeeming blood provoke agitation and blasphemous outbursts of fear in the affected subject. Sometimes the victim is described as speaking in another voice, or even another language. These signs are manifest. They should be distinguished from obsessive thoughts which, though they may be blasphemous or obscene, are symptoms common to psychiatric conditions and demonic manifestations. Of course the fact that the manifest signs are not features of recognized psychiatric illness does not mean that they could not be "explained" in psychological terms. It only means that something other than what we call psychiatric illness is implicated.

## Signs and Symptoms Common to Mental Illness and Demonic Influence

The number of such signs and symptoms is legion. They may concern the subject's volition — a lack of control so that (the person) performs actions which seem alien to him. He may experience violent swings of mood, inexplicable depressions, fears, hallucinatory voices or visions, suicidal or homicidal urges. There may be changes in his consciousness. He may appear to pass into fugue states or trances or to perform actions of which he seems to have no subsequent memory.

### Ephiphenomena

By ephiphenomena I mean things happening around (the person) — things that can be observed by other people like tappings, knockings, or unexplained movements of physical objects like the shaking of a bed or the transfer of china across a room. Such phenomena have been reported by many observers. Some of the phenomena have been subject to scientific investigation in an attempt to explore parapsychological hypotheses explaining them. Others have been recorded by newspaper reporters featuring poltergeist activities. They are uncommon, and more usually reported (at least if we read Christian literature) where there is a clear-cut history of previous occult practices (White in Montgomery, 1976).

Though the above criteria will be helpful in developing a "clinical picture" in discerning demonic activity, there is yet an additional basis for evaluation. This is the gift of the Holy Spirit for discerning or distinguishing spirits. The Apostle Paul mentions the gift of discerning spirit in 1 Corinthians 12:10. This spiritual gift is given to individual believers to be used in the context of the church. The person with this gift has the God-given ability to determine if the spirit operating on a person is demonic (spirit related), human, or divine (from the Holy Spirit).

> Discerning of Spirits is the supernatural capacity to judge from a spiritual insight whether the spirit operating has a source that is human, demonic, or divine. It is a supernatural perception into the spiritual activity realm for the purpose of determining the source of the spiritual activity. (John Wimber, Spiritual Gift Seminar, Vineyard Christian Fellowship)

God has not left His church without tools for discerning the work of His enemy and adversary, Satan. He has given His church the gift of discerning Spirits as well as the natural abilities of observation (the clinical picture) in determining the source of spirit world power.

## DEMON POSSESSION: A CASE STUDY

The case study for examination will be taken from the Bible. Of the many accounts of demon possession in the Bible, this account in the gospel of Mark of the Gerasene demoniac is certainly the most detailed in Scripture:

> And they came to the other side of the sea, into the country of the Gerasenes. And when He had come out of the boat, immediately a man from the tombs with an unclean spirit met Him, and he had his dwelling among the tombs; and no one was able to bind him any more, even with a chain; because he had often been bound with shackles and chains, and the chains had been torn apart by him, and the shackles broken in pieces, and no one was strong enough to subdue him. And constantly night and day,

among the tombs and in the mountains, he was crying out and gashing himself with stones.

And seeing Jesus from a distance, he ran up and bowed down before Him; and crying out with a loud voice, he said, "What do I have to do with You, Jesus, Son of the Most High God? I implore you by God, do not torment me!" For He had been saying to him, "Come out of the man, you unclean spirit!"

And He was asking him, "What is your name?" And he said to Him, "My name is Legion; for we are many." And he began to entreat Him earnestly not to send them out of the country.

Now there was a big herd of swine feeding there on the mountain side. And they entreated Him, saying, "Send us into the swine so that we may enter them." And He gave them permission. And coming out, the unclean spirits entered the swine; and the herd rushed down the steep bank into the sea, about two thousand of them; and they were drowned in the sea.

And those who tended them ran away and reported it in the city and out in the country. And the people came to see what it was that had happened. And they came to Jesus and observed the man who had been demon-possessed sitting down, clothed and in his right mind, the very man who had had the "legion;" and they became frightened. And those who had seen it described to them how it had happened to the demon-possessed man, and all about the swine.

Mark 5:1–16

# DEMONIZATION

This case study tells a great deal about demons and their relationship with Jesus and man.

**1. Demons are powerful.** Our text shows that this man had been given superhuman strength by which he could break chains and shackles. No one was able to control or subdue him.

**2. Demons are ultimately destructive.** This man under the control of demons was harming himself with stones. In the gospel of Matthew, we are given the added information that the demons "were so exceedingly violent that no one could pass by that road" (Matthew 8:28). Finally, this destructive bent is seen when the demons possessed the swine and they were immediately driven to destruction in the sea. The demons were destructive to the one possessed, to other people and even to animals.

**3. Demons know God.** When the demoniac saw Jesus at a distance, he knew that Jesus was the "Son of the Most High God." As was mentioned previously, demons know God because they initially stood in His presence as His loyal angels.

**4. Demons use God's name.** After the demoniac announced that he knew Jesus is the Son of God, he said, "I implore you by God, do not torment me." Demons know all of the tricks to try to get their own way. Perhaps a mere man would have been influenced by the use of God's name. But the Son of God knew that God's name had no power in the mouth of a demon.

**5. Demons recognize the authority of Jesus.** This is first seen as the demoniac ran up and bowed down to Jesus. The demons recognized that they were in the position of begging Jesus for mercy. They "implore" and then "entreat" Jesus not to send them away but to send them into the swine. They realized that Jesus could do with them as He pleased. Jesus had (and has) complete authority over demons.

**6. Demons are separate from the person.** Jesus did not deal with the man regarding his demons; He dealt with the demons regarding their man. Repeatedly, Jesus, and later the apostles, spoke directly to the demons as if the person who was possessed was merely a bystander.

**7. Demons are obedient to the authority of Jesus.** Jesus had commanded the demons to "come out of him, you unclean spirits." The demons knew that they would have to obey Jesus because He had commanded them to come out. The issue for the demons was not whether they would leave the man or not. The only issue was where Jesus would send them. They begged Jesus to send them into the swine, "and He gave them permission." Those demons came out just as Jesus had commanded and went into two thousand pigs which ran into the sea and were drowned.

## CASTING OUT DEMONS

Exorcism is the term that is often associated with casting out demons. This is not really a biblical term. It is used only once in Scripture to identify as "exorcists" the seven sons of Sceva who failed to cast out a demon. Though the term is not necessarily biblical, the principle is (Michaels in Montgomery 1976:57).

Casting out demons is a power encounter between God and the forces of Satan. Jesus said, "I cast out demons by the Spirit of God." Only God has sufficient power to cast out demons. However, it is seen in Scripture that Jesus granted this same authority to cast out demons to His followers (see Matthew 10:1 and Mark 6:7.) This power to cast out demons came from God whenever the disciples used the name of Jesus. As with the slave-girl possessed of the spirit of divination, the name of Jesus is called upon to cast out the demon. "I command you in the name of Jesus Christ to come out of her!" These words are used time and again in the casting out of demons.

However, it is not the words themselves which are somehow magically powerful for casting out demons. This lesson was learned by the seven brothers as told in Acts 19:13-16:

> But also some of the Jewish exorcists, who went from place to place, attempted to name over those who had the evil spirits the name of the Lord Jesus, saying, "I adjure you by Jesus whom Paul preaches." And seven sons of Sceva, a Jewish chief priest, were doing this. And the evil spirit answered and said to them, "I recognize Jesus and I know about Paul, but who are you?" And the man in whom was the evil spirit leaped on them and subdued both of them and overpowered them, so that they fled out of that house naked and wounded.

The above text shows that there is apparently a great deal more to casting out demons than the mere use of Jesus' name. The Pharisees at the time of Christ were active in exorcising demons (Matthew 12:27). However, theirs was a ritualistic exorcism. In the Philippines today, there are shamanistic exorcists who use occultic ritual to try to rid a person of spirit activity. (Sometimes the person who is afflicted with a demonic presence is simply tortured either mentally or physically so that they become an uncomfortable place for the possessing spirit to dwell). Even the Christian church often uses formula and ritual for exorcism. However, there is an inherent danger in the use of formula or ritual for exorcism.

> A ritualistic approach to overcoming demons seems to have inherent weakness of playing the devil's game by the devil's rules. It may be true that demons are subject to complex symbolic and ritualistic laws, but the Christian's authority does not spring from a manipulation of them (ritual being at best a "figure of the true") but from the very fountain of all authority. To depend on ritual for the

> exercise of power is to depend on magic. It undermines dependence on God (White in Montgomery 1976:296).

Casting out demons is the right of every believer through the exercise of his faith. This faith to cast out demons is focused on the position which the believer has in Christ and the power which he has in the Holy Spirit.

**1. Position.** The Apostle Paul carefully laid out for the believer his position and authority regarding the spirit world.

> ...These are in accordance with the working of the strength of His might which he brought about in Christ, when He raised Him from the dead, and seated Him at His right hand *in the heavenly places*, far above all rule and authority and power and dominion, and every name that is named, not only in this age, but also in the one to come. And He put all things in subjection under His feet, and gave Him as head over all things to the church, which is His body, the fullness of Him who fills all in all.
> Ephesians 1:19–23 (emphasis supplied)

> But God, being rich in mercy, because of His great love with which He loved us, even when we were dead in our transgressions, made us alive together with Christ (by grace you have been saved), and raised us up with Him, and seated us with Him *in the heavenly places*, in Christ Jesus.
> Ephesians 2:4–6 (emphasis supplied)

Paul states that God raised Jesus from the dead to a position "in the heavenly places" above all other rule and authority (especially that of Satan). Then God raised the believer from the death of sin and put him "in the heavenly places" in Christ who is above all other rule and authority. Therefore, the believer has the same position and authority over Satan and his demons as that enjoyed by Jesus Christ.

**2. Power.** The power which a believer has comes from the Holy Spirit. Man has no power of his own with which to do battle against Satan. The power which the believer possesses to exercise his authority and position in Christ comes from God through the Holy Spirit. Acts 1:8 states it clearly: "But you shall receive power when the Holy Spirit has come upon you."

All spiritual warfare, including casting out demons, will be successful if the believer recognizes the position he has in Christ and the power he has in the Holy Spirit over all other authority including, and especially, that of Satan.

> Effective exorcism does not depend on permission from a church hierarchy or the authority of any senior churchman. Nor is any specific formula of service or prayer required. It is not even necessary in exorcism to have the victim's approval. The possessed is often not in a position to understand what is going on. But success in exorcism does depend on the intent and faith of two or three who pray in the name of Jesus Christ. We can only have glimpses of God's purposes and we can only dimly comprehend the mysteries underlying these events. We step out in faith with a profound, non-rationalistic conviction of the truth of the proposition. Christ commanded us to preach, heal, and cast out evil, and this apparently we can do with effectiveness far beyond our human understanding. We have proved the truth that the grace of our Lord is adequate for every situation. Taste and see! (White in Montgomery 1976:277).

Deliverance from demonic possession involves more than casting out demons. Biblical deliverance is only complete when the person is delivered from his bondage to sin through a *born again* experience. Complete deliverance comes when a person is saved by grace through faith (Ephesians 2:8,9). He is then delivered "from the domain of darkness" and transferred "to the kingdom of His beloved Son" (Colossians 1:13). This salvation from the kingdom of darkness whose king is Satan gives the believer the position and power which is described above, so that he can resist the devil and his angels and help others who are caught in the "domain of darkness."

## DEMONIC OPPRESSION OR SUBJECTION

It is an error to think of demonic activity only in terms of demonic possession. There is demonic activity which can afflict a person and yet show none of the symptoms and signs of possession. Some have called this lesser demonic activity *demon oppression* or *subjection*.

> The marks of demon possession are very extreme and quite rare. Demon subjection is perhaps more common. The marks of demon subjection are much less extreme than demon possession. Alfred Lechler suggests some of the characteristics of demon subjection: non-receptivity to divine things, religious doubt, inaptness for true knowledge of sin, inability to concentrate in Bible reading and prayer, persistent lack of peace, inner unrest, temper bursts, blasphemy, depression, and suicidal thoughts. With these is joined various compulsions toward drunkenness, sexual immorality, falsehood, theft, smoking and drugs (Mallory in Montgomery 1976:340).

Oppression differs from possession in the degree of control exercised by the demon and given up by the person being oppressed. Oppression is demonic control in which the personality and character of the person oppressed is still present. With possession, the person gives up his personality and will for that of the demon.

## DEMONIC INFLUENCE

Believers often find it difficult to imagine that Satan could possibly have any power or influence in their lives. They see their inner lives as fortresses which cannot be penetrated by the forces of evil.

> I suggest that a significant degree of emotional immaturity, distress and even nervous breakdowns among Evangelicals could be traced to this utopian error. Convinced that his inner life cannot be satanically worked upon, that only the Holy Spirit can possibly influence him within, the Evangelical tries to keep up an "I'm so happy" façade which contradicts his real experience and drives him to hypocrisy at best, psychic collapse at worst. Theologically, it deflects him from the one proper recourse: constant return in penitence to the cross of Christ (Montgomery 1976:234).

Certainly, Peter was a man who had spiritual insight and knowledge and yet he experienced satanic influence as seen in Matthew 16. At Caesaria Philippi, Jesus asked His disciples, "Who do you say that I am?" (v.15). To this question Peter answered, "Thou art the Christ, the Son of the Living God" (v.16). Jesus responded that this had come to Peter as revelation. "Blessed are you, Simon Barjonas, because flesh and blood did not reveal this to you, but My Father who is in heaven" (v.17). Certainly this is enough evidence to indicate that Peter had been inspired by God.

Jesus continued to reveal more of Himself to Peter and the other disciples in the same chapter of Matthew. He told them that He must go to Jerusalem to suffer and die. Peter did not like this plan at all so he took Jesus aside and "began to rebuke Him" (v.22). To this Jesus utters to Peter some of the most astounding words of Scripture, "Get behind Me, Satan! You are a stumbling block to Me; for you are not setting your mind on God's interests, but man's" (v. 23).

It seems as though Jesus was addressing both Satan and Peter. Though Peter had just finished his great confession of Jesus as the Christ, he came under the influence of Satan, so that Jesus addressed Satan as the source of Peter's idea. This influence was, of course, directed to the mind of Peter who had apparently set his mind on the interests of man and not on the interests of God. Here, we see an example of divine revelation and satanic influence in the same man, Peter.

## DEMONIC TEMPTATION

The lowest level of demonic or satanic activity which is common to the unbeliever, the believer, and to Jesus Christ while He was here on earth, is temptation. Scripture tells us that Jesus was tempted by Satan in all the ways that man has been tempted, "yet without sin" (Hebrews 4:15). None can escape the demonic activity of temptation, not even the Lord Jesus Christ.

Satan and his demons cleverly act upon man's thoughts and desires. When they find something that is slightly out of God's will, they intensify it until it becomes a full-blown passion and sin. They inject more fantasies, feelings, and sensations which are not part of a person's normal experience or character (Mallory in Montgomery 1976:337).

The subtlety of temptation is based on the fact that Satan often uses very normal and natural "everyday concerns" and distorts their importance. In this way natural appetites become unnatural obsessions so that man is distracted from his relationship with God.

> Clearly both Christians and non-Christians are subject to the ordinary influences of the satanic world order. Through the intermediate means of the fleshly nature within, and

> the corrupted world around, suggestions occur to us contrary to God's pleasure and revealed will. Temptations strike at the heart of our relation to God and His purposes.
> (Mallory in Montgomery 1976:359)

## SPIRITUAL WARFARE AND GOD'S ARMOR

In fighting the satanic and demonic forces of influence and temptation, the believer calls upon his position in Christ and the power of the Holy Spirit. Once again, the key element in this struggle is faith.

> ...And this is the victory that has overcome the world — our faith.
> 1 John 5:4

This faith also overcomes the god of this world, Satan.

Paul clearly states that man's struggle is against the powers and rulers of darkness, whom we know to be Satan and his demons. In this battle, God has given the believer His strength and a full set of armor so that he can be successful in this struggle.

> Finally, build up your strength in union with the Lord and by means of his mighty power. Put on all the armor that God gives you, so that you will be able to stand up against the Devil's evil tricks. For we are not fighting against human beings but against the wicked spiritual forces in the heavenly world, the rulers, authorities, and cosmic powers of this dark age.
> Ephesians 6:10-13 *TEV*

Paul goes on in the same text of Scripture to list the various pieces which make up God's armor for the believer. They include truth, righteousness, peace, faith, salvation, and the

Word of God. Each piece of God's armor has a very important role to play in the believer's battle against Satan. It is important to know how to put the armor on and how to use it everyday so that when the battles come — and they will — the believer will be able to use it successfully. The key to the successful use of God's armor is prayer. Prayer provides the vehicle through which the Holy Spirit demonstrates His power in the believer's life and through the believer's lives to others.

Though Satan has a vast army of demons at his disposal, God is not powerless to deal with the situation. God has an army of angels twice the size of Satan's army which He has sent out to the aid of His children. Demons are spirit beings whose power is far beyond that of man. But God has granted to His followers the authority, position, and power over Satan and his demons so that they can resist and cast out the Evil One "in the name of Jesus Christ."

# 8
# DISCERNING SUPERNATURAL POWERS

There is confusion among many Christian Filipinos when they are confronted with what they perceive to be spirit world problems of demon possession and spirit-caused sickness.

Since the Filipino *in-church* religion of ultimate concerns does not address itself to a *this worldly* spirit world, some very important aspects of the spirit world are left to their *out-of-church* belief system and practitioners. The three most important areas which are *out-of-church* are illness, divination, and problems with spirits (possession, curses, certain types of sickness, *buyag*, etc.). With the exception of Pentecostals and Charismatics, these are generally not dealt with or taken seriously by the church

Consequently, the Filipino Christian both Catholic and Protestant alike will go to those who are mediators and practitioners of the spirit world in these matters of illness, problems with spirits, and divination. They are forced to go out of church in these matters because they think that it is not "the business of the church" to handle them.

## REACTION OF *IN-CHURCH* LEADERS TO *OUT-OF-CHURCH* PRACTITIONERS

Filipino church leaders are divided as to the source of power of these spirit world practitioners to whom Christians are going to for help. The more western element would say that these practitioners have no power; they simply use psychology and trickery. Others would say that these people really do have power but that power comes from Satan and his demons.

Most Filipino Christians do not accept either of these explanations. In countless interviews, it was revealed that most Filipinos believe that the power to work miracles of healing, resolving troubles with spirits, and divination comes from God. Their judgment as to the source of power of the spirit world practitioners is based on whether the results of their work are good or evil. So the practitioners who perform miracles for man's good is seen to get their power from God.

These practitioners of the *this worldly* spirit world all claim God as their source of power. To further support the belief that their power comes from God, they live pious lives. They regularly go to church and claim to spend a great deal of time in prayer. Their homes are full of religious objects and their conversation is full of religious terminology. All of these things convince most Filipinos that these practitioners of the spirit world are godly men whose power comes from God.

This leaves most Filipino Christians a belief system, in which God is seen working through *in-church* practitioners in matters of ultimate concern, and through *out-of-church* practitioners in matters of everyday concerns: illness, troubles with spirits, and divination.

Unless directly confronted, *in-church* leaders will ignore the existence and problems of the spirit world. They simply pretend that there is no issue or problem, or that it is a problem for only a selected few who are on the fringes of the church anyway.

When church leaders are directly confronted with the issues of the spirit world, they generally condemn the practice of their members going to the *mananambal* or spirit world practitioner. They do so because they condemn the practitioners as either fake or demonic. They see that going to a *mananambal* for a cure would be inconsistent with a believer's faith in God.

Church leaders want to condemn the practices of the *out-of-church* beliefs of these people without clear teaching on the subject. They believe that their condemnation of these *out-of-church* spirit world practitioners will stop their members from going to them. This is not the case. The condemnation simply results in the "conspiracy of silence" on this subject. With silence on the subject, the church leaders believe that the problem is solved. The members interpret the same silence to mean that the church has no concern in this matter.

Church leaders want to condemn practitioners of the spirit world without giving their members an alternative. It does no good to tell a person not to go to a *mananambal* because it is wrong. When a person believes that he is being troubled by a spirit, a condemning word from a church leader will not stop him. Such a person will seek relief from his spirit problem in one way or another. Unless the church provides clear teaching on the subject of the spirit world and its practitioners, as well as providing alternatives to going to such practitioners, the problem will continue as it has in the past.

## ARE THESE *OUT-OF-CHURCH* PRACTICES A PROBLEM?

It is not fully agreed that these *out-of-church* practices are a real problem for the church. The Roman Catholic Church leaders are very much aware of these *out-of-church* practices much more so than Protestant church leaders. As long as these practices do not interfere directly with the teachings of the Catholic Church, they will be tolerated.

The Roman Catholic Church calls this tolerance of the culture and practices of the people "accommodation." The Roman Catholic anthropologist, Dr. Louis Luzbetak, defines accommodation as "the respectful, prudent, scientifically and theologically sound adjustment of the church to the native culture in attitude, outward behavior, and practical apostolic approach" (1970:341). This policy of accommodation, while a good missiological principle, has led to a great deal of mixture because Catholic church leaders were not as discerning as they should have been about the animist practices of Filipinos.

There seems to be a bit of inconsistency on the part of the Catholic Church regarding many of the *out-of-church* practices of its members. The Catholic church leadership (bishops and higher) regards such *out-of-church* practices as foolishness, ignorance and superstition, while many of the local priests, especially the rural priests, ignore or even condone these things.

The official policy of the Roman Catholic Church is that the statues and sacred objects have no power in and of themselves. Yet the local parish leadership encourages this belief by making claims of miraculous cures brought about by the *Santo Niño* or the Black Nazarene. Long lines of people can be seen daily waiting to touch the glass which encloses the *Santo Niño* statue in the belief that they can obtain healing and protection by simply touching the glass.

Official church dogma and policy make no claims about the power of palm branches in the shape of a cross to ward off spirits. However, local church priests continue to bless them every year on Palm Sunday.

So it seems clear that the higher church leadership recognizes the potential problems of folk Catholicism while the local church leaders are quite tolerant and "understanding."

On the other hand, the Protestant church leaders, especially western missionaries, would be very concerned about the *out-of-church* practices of their members, but they are unaware of the situation because of the "conspiracy of silence." These church leaders preach, teach, and counsel without mention of a *this worldly* spirit world and its practitioners, because they are not confronted with the issue by their members. *In-church* practitioners do not want confrontation on this subject because they have no tools or theology to handle these types of situations. The members no longer confront the leaders for fear of being labeled "superstitious" or even "demonic."

Many Filipino church members (both Catholic and Protestant) see no real conflict in going to their *in-church* practitioners for ultimate concerns and to their *out-of-church* practitioners for everyday concerns. The issue is simply one of specialization. If the problem is sin, it is necessary to go to an *in-church* practitioner such as a pastor or priest who specializes in ultimate concerns. But if the problem is perceived to be a *da-ut* (a curse), then it is necessary to go to an *out-of-church* practitioner who specializes in a *this worldly* spirit world. In the same way, if the problem is a broken watch, it should be taken to one who specializes in watch repair. There is no perceived conflict because each category is separate and specialized. The *in-church* practitioners — pastors and priests — have little or no teaching on the subject of the *this worldly* spirit world, so members assume that this does not fall under the concern of the church.

In spite of this, these *out-of-church* practices could provide real problems for believers and for the church. The Filipinization of the church will require bringing the Bible to bear on all *out-of-church* practices to see if they are consistent with the Word of God.

## DISCERNING THE PRACTITIONERS OF GOD

The danger of Filipino Christians going to *out-of-church* practitioners stems from the fact that they can be exposing themselves to powers and spirits which are not of God. Discerning which of the *out-of-church* practitioners is using the power of God is not an easy task. Actually, the task is not the discernment of practitioners of power. Rather, the task is the discernment of the spirit who is the practitioner's source of power.

Missionaries and national church leaders have little difficulty in passing judgment on virtually all *out-of-church* practitioners. For those who have no belief in a *this worldly* spirit world, all *out-of-church* practitioners are frauds who prey on the superstition of ignorant people. For those missionaries and Filipino church leaders who have some awareness of *this worldly* spirit world, these practitioners are getting their power from Satan. In either event, missionaries and Filipino church leaders tell their church members that going to *out-of-church* practitioners is either demonic or ignorant superstition.

Most Filipino Christians do not share this evaluation of *out-of-church* practitioners. However, they do evaluate *out-of-church* practitioners as to their source of power. Those *out-of-church* practitioners who use sorcery to bring sickness or even death to other people are clearly seen as having a "devil spirit." However, those *out-of-church* practitioners who use "their" power to heal the sick or divine the future are believed to get their power from God. The major criterion for the Filipino in judging *out-of-church* practitioners is whether the results are good or bad for man.

Most Filipinos believe in the claims of the *out-of-church* practitioners who maintain that their power comes from God.

The examination of three texts of Scripture may help in seeing if the results, the reputation, or the claims of the *out-of-church* practitioner of power are good bases for judging his source of power.

## THE MAGIC OF SIMON, THE SORCERER

The first of these texts deals with a magician who was a practitioner of spirit world power.

> Now there was a certain man named Simon, who formerly was practicing magic in the city, and astonishing the people of Samaria, claiming to be someone great;

> and they all, from smallest to greatest, were giving attention to him saying, "This man is what is called the Great Power of God." And they were giving him attention because he had for a long time astonished them with his magic arts. But when they believed Philip preaching the good news about the kingdom of God and the name of Jesus Christ, they were being baptized, men and women alike. And even Simon himself believed; and after being baptized, he continued on with Philip; and as he observed signs and great miracles taking place, he was constantly amazed.
>
> Now when Simon saw that the Spirit was bestowed through the laying on of the apostles' hands, he offered them money, saying, "Give this authority to me as well, so that everyone on whom I lay my hands may receive the Holy Spirit. But Peter said to him, "May your silver perish with you, because you thought you could obtain the gift of God with money! You have no part or portion in this matter, for your heart is not right before God."
>
> Acts 8:9–13 and 18–21

There are several lessons to be learned from this text regarding power and practitioners of power.

1. The source of Simon's power is questionable, it may be evil or demonic. Simon truly worked many miracles for the people of Samaria, but the above texts call them "magic."

Today the word "magic" has a different meaning than it had in Bible times. Today magic is performed on stage or television as a skill which uses illusions and sleight of hand to entertain. But magic can also mean the use of formulas, rituals, or incantations to control the power of the spirit world (Grant 1982:58). In biblical times, magic was the source of power and knowledge for controlling elements of the spirit world.

The story of Moses, Aaron and Pharaoh illustrates what the Bible means by magic. When Moses went to Pharaoh with Aaron, he performed miracles before Pharaoh to show God's power. Aaron threw down his shepherd's staff before Pharaoh and it turned into a serpent. The "magicians of Egypt" (Exodus 7:11) also threw down their staffs and these, too, became serpents; but Aaron's serpent swallowed the other serpents. Aaron stretched out his staff over the Nile river and God turned it to blood. "But the magicians of Egypt did the same with their secret arts" (Exodus 7:22). The magicians of Egypt had real power which was called "magic arts" in the Bible. This power was like the power of God, but it was used against the purposes of God. Arthur Glasser suggests that, "in this case, Pharaoh embodied all the demonic forces of resistance" (1982:36).

Simon used his magic to control the spirit world and work miracles which appeared to come from God. But God cannot be controlled because He is the Sovereign Ruler of the universe. Therefore, it is possible that Simon did not get his power from God.

Finally, the Bible says that God gives His power to believers through the Holy Spirit (Acts 2:38 and Acts 1:8). Simon was working these miracles before he heard and believed the message of Jesus Christ. He was performing miracles while he was still an unbeliever. This power may not have come from God.

2. The source of Simon's power was at least questionable, yet "all" the people of Samaria, "from the smallest to the greatest," believed that his power to work miracles came from God. They called him "the Great Power of God." He astonished them with the miracles.

3. Simon and the people of Samaria were power-oriented rather than Christ-oriented. After Simon believed and was baptized he saw that the power of the apostles was much greater than what he had previously known in magic. He wanted this

ability to be given by the Holy Spirit and offered Peter money in exchange for this power. Simon was power-oriented, but the apostle Peter was person-oriented, saying "your heart is not right before God."

It is so difficult to determine the source of power by just looking at the manifestations of that power. The power itself and even its results (miracles) are poor bases for judging the source of power.

Simon was a magician who worked his miracles using the magical arts. The results of these miracles had the people from far and near believing that God was the source of his power, which was not the case. He had a reputation as being the "great power of God," and yet he did not even know the God of salvation until later in his life. So the results of miracles, and the reputation of the miracle worker, do not provide a sound basis for judging the source of power.

## False Prophets: Wolves in Sheep's Clothing

In this second text for examination Jesus warns about the existence of "false prophets" who have the power to work miracles, cast out demons, and prophesy.

> Beware of the false prophets, who come to you in sheep's clothing, but inwardly are ravenous wolves
> Matthew 7:15

> Not everyone who says to Me, "Lord, Lord" will enter the kingdom of heaven; but he who does the will of My Father, who is in heaven. Many will say to Me on that day, Lord, Lord, did we not prophesy in Your Name, and in Your name cast out demons, and in Your name perform many miracles?" And then I will declare to them, "I never knew you, depart from Me, you who practice lawlessness."
> Matthew 7:21–23

These are powerful words from the mouth of Jesus about power and deception. All of the things that these false prophets did were good. The miracles, prophecy, and casting out demons were not wrong. These were the very same things which the apostles did. All of these manifestations of supernatural power were done in the name of Jesus. The false prophets did not hesitate to give God the credit for the power to work miracles.

But Jesus would have none of it. He could see through the miracles and the claims of the false prophets, and see their hearts. To these miracle workers Jesus proclaimed, "I never knew you, depart from Me." The power to do all of these "wonderful" things did not come from God but from Satan. They were good things done in the name of Jesus but still Jesus said "I never knew you." Indeed, they had all the appearances of having the "Great power of God," but they were "ravenous wolves" wearing "sheep's clothing."

Man can be easily fooled by power. The "sheep's clothing" of these miracle workers is a disguise to cover their real source of power. This disguise can come in the form of Christian language and appearance of Christian piety. However, the fact that a person works miracles in the name of Jesus for the good of mankind does not necessarily mean that the power comes from God.

As we have seen in a previous chapter, Satan is also powerful and deceptive. He is the master counterfeiter of God's work. It is his desire to attract man to power so that he will be distracted from the Person of Jesus Christ. Like Simon the magician, man is attracted to power. God wants man to be attracted to Him, while Satan wants to distract man by seducing him with power.

Again, the beneficial results of the miracles and the claims that their power comes from God is not a basis for judgment as to the source of power of *out-of-church* practitioners. Jesus said that some would cast out demons, prophesy, and work miracles in His name, yet He did not know them.

## THE "SHEEP'S CLOTHING" OF RIGHTEOUSNESS

In the final text, Paul also warns that these false prophets, who are wolves, maybe wearing "sheep's clothing" of righteousness.

> For such men are false apostles, deceitful workers, disguising themselves as apostles of Christ. And no wonder, for even Satan disguises himself as an angel of light. Therefore it is not surprising if his servants also disguise themselves as servants of righteousness...
> 2 Corinthians 11:13-15

That the king of darkness should come to man "as an angel of light" shows all too well the cleverness of Satan. But to further deceive man, his servants (those who carry out Satan's will) appear to man as "servants of righteousness." Their power looks like the power of God. Their miracles are done in the name of Jesus. These servants of Satan may look like pious people of God. They may have reputations as persons of prayer and high moral standards, but this is only the "sheep's clothing" which disguises these servants of Satan, who gives them their counterfeiting power. This is frightening but true.

The *out-of-church* practitioners of the spirit world to whom Christians go to for help *may be* servants of Satan. They may claim to get their power from God for the good of man. However, they *may be* getting their power from Satan.

## Testing the Power of the Spirit World

It is very difficult to determine if a practitioner of the spirit world who is performing miracles gets his power from God or Satan. From the Bible, the distinction cannot be made in the miracles themselves, the credit given to God as the source of power, or the apparent "righteousness" of the person.

### Is the Gospel message present?

The Lord Jesus said, referring to false prophets, that you can tell a tree by its fruit. "Even so every good tree bears good fruit; but the rotten tree bears bad fruit" (Matthew 7:17). The "good fruit" that He is talking about here is a fruit which cannot be counterfeited by Satan. It is not external like the words and actions of the person with the power. The test of good fruit in the person working the miracles is this: Does his power point people to a relationship with God through Jesus?

The miracles of Jesus were done to show the world that He was the Son of God. The miracles that the apostles worked were a testimony that their message about Jesus Christ was true. They attested to the fact that God had come to man to provide a relationship in which the believer was "in Christ;" that the Holy Spirit was in the believer. Miracles went hand in hand with bringing man into a right relationship with God through Jesus Christ. This is the "good fruit" which the apostles produced with the miracles from God's power.

Jesus explains how fruit is produced in an illustration about a vine and its branches. In this text, Jesus starts by calling Himself "The Vine." Then He tells how the branches can bear fruit.

> Abide in Me, and I in you. As the branch cannot bear fruit of itself, unless it abides in the vine, so neither can you, unless you abide in Me. I am the vine, you are the

> branches; he who abides in Me, and I in him, he bears much fruit; for apart from Me you can do nothing.
> John 15:4–5

The only way to bear "good fruit" is by "abiding" in Jesus. Any servant of God who is using His power will show people the way to this abiding relationship with God through Jesus. Miracles were always performed as a sign that God loves man and wants to know him in a relationship.

Servants of Satan will not show people the way to God through Jesus Christ. Those false prophets who are working miracle and disguising themselves "as servants of righteousness" may give the people a great deal of "Christian talk" but they will not show the way to a saving relationship with God through Jesus Christ. They may encourage someone to pray or go to church or live a better life, but they will not show anyone the way to salvation. They will be clever with their words so that they sound Christian, but the complete message of salvation by faith in Jesus Christ will be missing.

Satan wants to keep mankind from a faith relationship with God through Jesus Christ. He will do anything, and use anyone, to distract people from the gospel message.

> The primary manifestation of satanic influence and of the evil of This Age is religious; it is blindness with reference to the Gospel of Jesus Christ (Ladd 1981:31).

The task of distinguishing between the miracles of God and those of Satan is a very difficult one indeed. The task is of a spiritual nature which requires measuring the words and actions of the practitioner of power against what one knows about the words and actions of Jesus.

> Beloved, do not believe every spirit, but test the spirits to see whether they are from God; because many false prophets have gone out into the world. By this you know

> the Spirit of God: every spirit that confesses that Jesus Christ has come in the flesh is from God; and every spirit that does not confess Jesus is not from God...
> 1 John 4:1-3

The spirits of these practitioners of power must be tested against God's message of salvation by grace through faith (Ephesians 2:8,9). The miracles of God are worked within the context of this message. If the practitioner of power is not proclaiming this message from God, then there is serious reason to doubt the source of his power.

## Miracles in the name of which Jesus?

In the Philippines and around the world, there are many miracles which are worked "in the name of Jesus." To simply use the name "Jesus" does not mean that these miracle workers are referring to the Jesus of the Bible. The Apostle Paul recognizes this in his warning to the church at Corinth:

> But I am afraid, lest as the serpent deceived Eve by his craftiness, your minds should be led astray from the simplicity and purity of devotion to Christ. For if one comes and preaches another Jesus whom we have not preached, or you receive a *different spirit* which you have not received, or a *different gospel* which you have not accepted, you bear this beautifully.
> 2 Corinthians 11:3,4 (emphasis supplied)

Paul stresses that the church must guard itself against the craftiness of Satan. This craftiness of Satan has one goal: that believers "be led astray" from their "devotion to Christ." This is done by Satan through those who come with "another Jesus," "another spirit" and "another gospel."

Miracles can be performed. Demons can be cast out, and prophecy can be uttered. All of these can be done in the name of Jesus but still be demonic in nature. Jesus Himself warns about this in Matthew 7:22,23. To these miracle workers, He said "I never knew you; *Depart from Me, you who practice lawlessness.*" These people may use the name of Jesus, but it is not the Jesus of the Bible because He does not know them.

Johanna Michaelsen spent several years as the assistant to a famous psychic healer in Mexico. During that time she fully believed that the power to work those healing miracles came from God. She later discovered that the power came from Satan. In her book, *The Beautiful Side of Evil,* she tells of discovering the demonic source power which manifests itself in ways that appear to be beneficial to mankind. Her first test is "Which Jesus?"

> The first test of a prophet (or healer) must be in the area of doctrine: What does he believe about Jesus? Does he cling to Jesus Christ of Nazareth as God the Son; Second Person of the Trinity; God incarnate in human flesh; the God-Man who died upon the cross in our place for the forgiveness of our sins; the One born of a Virgin whose physical resurrection from the dead proclaimed His victory over sin, death and Satan? Does that person believe it is "by grace you have been saved through faith; and that not of yourselves, it is the gift of God; not as a result of works, that no one should boast?" (Ephesians 2:8,9). Or have they, through subtle redefinition, come to accept "another Jesus," "another spirit," "another gospel?" (1982:196).

In her experience with the spirit world, she was often visited by what she taught was the Jesus of the Bible. She later discovered that she had been visited by a demonic spirit who called himself "Jesus." Perhaps, this is what the Apostle is referring to when he speaks of "another Jesus."

## Testing diviners with the tests of a prophet

Diviners provide to their clients information which is not available from natural means. This information is supplied to the diviner from the spirit world. The client goes to the diviner because of anxiety over his future. The diviner is paid to give the client information about the future so that the client can make better decisions in the present.

The future or fortune-telling aspect of diviners is somewhat parallel to part of the task of Old Testament prophets. These prophets would often proclaim the future, but this would be done in the context of calling the people to repentance. *Unger's Bible Dictionary* defines an Old Testament prophet as one "divinely inspired to communicate God's will and to disclose the future to them" (Unger 1961:890).

How to discern prophets of God from false prophets was a problem for the children of Israel even in the time of Moses. God gives Moses, the children of Israel, and people of today, the test for determining whether God is the source of knowledge and power of the person telling the future.

> You may wonder how you can tell when a prophet's message does not come from the Lord. If a prophet speaks in the name of the Lord and what he says does not come true, then it is not the Lord's message. That prophet has spoken on his own authority, and you are not to fear him.
>
> Deuteronomy 18:21, 22, TEV

The test of the diviner is not based on how we feel about him or what he says nor on his reputation or lifestyle. If a diviner is getting his information about the future from God, then it will be one hundred percent correct. After all, God does not make mistakes.

Finally, prophecy or future-telling in the Bible is given in the context of a message of repentance or salvation. The prophets of the Old Testament told the future but at the same time called the people of Israel to repentance. New Testament prophecy regarding the last days tells of the future for those who are saved and for those who are not. Again, there is implied message of salvation within the context of telling the future.

The element of the salvation message will be conspicuously absent with diviners. They are not concerned to bring people to repentance and to faith in God. In fact, the diviner is concerned to have people put their faith in him and his power to tell the future. This faith in the diviner and his spirit is a distraction from faith in God.

It is not an easy task to evaluate the source of power of *out-of-church* practitioners. However, from our examination of Scripture, it should be apparent that they cannot be evaluated by the miracles they work, their pious reputations, or their claims of power from God. The biblical tests focus on the gospel message. Do these *out-of-church* practitioners use their power in the context of leading people to salvation through faith in Christ? And are they using the name of the Jesus Christ of the Bible, who died on the cross? In the matter of divination, those who claim to tell the future by the power of God must be completely accurate every time. Those are the biblical tests of Scripture regarding practitioners of power. Yet there is one more very important test which focuses on the very essence of Christianity. This is the test of trust.

# 9
# THE TEST OF TRUST

This chapter will focus on the relationship between Christian believers and *out-of-church* practitioners of the spirit world. The force of the argument presented hinges on the very definition of a Christian. There is an institutional definition and a dynamic definition.

The institutional definition of Christianity is that the church, as an institution, is God's vehicle of grace to His people. This grace is administered through the church in the sacraments. Failure to perform the functions of the church will hinder the flow of God's blessings. A Christian is one who rightly performs the functions of the church.

A dynamic definition of Christianity puts the individual and his trust (faith) relationship with God at the center of the definition. The grace of God is given to the individual believer, primarily through fellow believers within the church. God's blessings are hindered by a violation of this trust relationship. A Christian is one who has a trust relationship with God through Jesus Christ.

It is this dynamic definition of Christianity which will be the focus of our final and most important test of the believer in relation to spirit world practitioners.

*The Test of Trust*

## Trusting the Spirits

A trust relationship is easily developed between a person who has a need and another person who can meet that need. This is the case between a medical doctor and his patients. The patient goes to the doctor because he trusts the knowledge of the doctor to make him well. Trust is a necessary element in the doctor-patient relationship. The doctor hears things with the stethoscope which the patient cannot hear, and feels things with his hands which the patient cannot feel. Finally, the doctor writes some medical terms on a piece of paper which the patient cannot understand. All of this requires a great deal of trust in the doctor and in his knowledge of medicine.

This same type of trust relationship is established between the *out-of-church* spirit world practitioner and his clients. These practitioners of the *this worldly* spirit world have power and knowledge which the average person does not understand. This power and knowledge comes to them from their spirit mentors. These spirit mentors are said to be the spirits of the dead, the saints, the Virgin Mary, or even Christ Himself. The spirits often give the practitioner both the diagnosis and the method of cure. So the spirit is both the power behind the diagnosis as well as the cure.

> *Mananambals* have special, personal relationships with spiritual benefactors whose power can be utilized to serve the needs of the *mananambal's* clients and patients. In the Cebuano area, patrons of the *mananambal* include spirits of deceased *mananambal*, saints, Christ, and God. Often the *mananambal's* most important methods for diagnosing and treating illnesses are those about which his spiritual mentor has informed him in dreams or visions, in some instances, the mentor may diagnose and prescribe treatment for the illness of each patient of the *mananambal*. And the *mananambal* generally seeks more

> than information from his spiritual benefactor. He also tries to enlist the force of his benefactor into the treatment through prayer and utilization of symbols associated with his benefactor. No matter who the spiritual backer of the *mananambal* is and how the *mananambal's* connection with him is demonstrated and used, this connection offers the *mananambal* access to a source of extraordinary power (Lieban 1977:31).

Since this spirit world information is out of reach of the average person, the client must trust the practitioner's knowledge of the future. Since this knowledge of the future comes from a spirit, he is ultimately putting his trust in the spirit. As with the practitioner of medicine, the client must trust the knowledge of the *mananambal* without understanding what is going on.

Two of the Philippines' most famous "psychic healers" of the past years are described as having spirits, or spirit beings that inform them and give them their power to perform these miracles.

> Terte operates only when spirits inform him they will be ready, then he handles a number of cases within a relatively short time. . . I saw quite a number of operations after this. At no time during any of them did the patient show any sign of pain. . . I know these operations were real. I was there. I handled the tissues removed from the patients. I smelled the decay of diseased organs. I saw the flesh that was instantaneously healed. I cannot explain what I have seen, although I feel there is an explanation for this somewhere (Sherman 1967:12).

> He (Tony Agpaoa) would have lived an ordinary life, on the farm, had it not been, at the age of nine, that a spiritual experience came to him in the form of what he calls

> a "Protector," about whom he has been instructed not to say too much...This invisible "Protector" is always present, so I understand, at his operations...He is rather hesitant to talk about any reference to the "Protector" and prefers to call it "the God power" which I think is in good taste... Anyway, this "invisible cosmic presence," whatever it is, must be a powerful entity, living on another plane of existence, an intelligent being with some plan for mankind (Sherman 1967:26).

With the medical practitioner and with the spirit world practitioner, the patient is ultimately putting his trust in the source of knowledge which brings the cure. With the doctor, the patient is ultimately putting his trust in medical science. With the spirit world practitioner, the client is ultimately putting his trust in the spirit who provides for the diagnosis and the cure.

This same kind of trust relationship is established with spirit world practitioners who specialize in divination. The client will trust the knowledge of the diviner to such an extent that he will use the diviner's information from the spirit world for many areas of his life. One such client related the following as an example of this trust relationship with a diviner.

> My husband called the diviner the other day and the diviner told him not to do his business on Monday because it would not be a good day for him. He was right because that day, the car we were riding was hit from behind, and our son got sick. My husband also asked him when we should move into our home and he gave us a date based on the moon. So we will be moving next Wednesday (Henry 1983:b).

It is apparent that the client must have a great deal of trust in the diviner in order to base many financial and family decisions on the information which he gives. Ultimately, however, the trust that the client has is in the source of knowledge of the diviner, the spirit world, and not in the diviner himself.

From the previous discussions about the source of power of the spirit world practitioners, it is apparent that, at best, their source of power is unknown, and very possibly could be demonic. It is impossible to base a judgment of their source of power on the miracles themselves, on the fact that they are good for man, or on the life of the practitioner. If their power does come from Satan and his demons, then to go to that practitioner would be to put trust in Satan in the matters of healing, spirit problems or divination.

## GOD IS JEALOUS

The Bible tells of a holy God who sits on the throne of the universe. This powerful, sovereign God loves man and desires that He and man have a loving relationship based on faith. This is the foremost desire in God's heart. God reacts against anything which might threaten His relationships with those who trust Him. This reaction is jealousy.

Jealousy is often thought of as a negative attitude that should not be attributed to anyone and most certainly not to God. Humans are very familiar with jealousy as it often relates to a romantic relationship between a man and a woman. A woman maybe jealous of another person or thing that affects her relationship with the man she loves. But for jealousy to be justified, there must first be a commitment between the man and woman, such as marriage or engagement. When this commitment is made, jealousy is understood as the feeling which guards the relationship against all rivals. A woman can be jealous of another woman who is trying to steal her husband or fiancé. She may be jealous of basketball because her husband spends more time playing basketball than being with her.

> I am the LORD your God, who brought you out of the land of Egypt, out of the house of slavery. You shall have no other gods before Me. You shall not make for yourself an idol, or any likeness of what is in heaven above or on the earth beneath or in the water under the earth. You shall not worship them or serve them; for I, the LORD your God, am a jealous God.
> Exodus 20:2–5

This is quoted from the first of God's Ten Commandments, written by His finger on tablets of stone. The first commandment states beyond all doubt that God is a jealous God. As man's Creator, He feels that man owes Him honor and allegiance. As man's Savior, He feels that man owes Him love and trust. God has done everything to provide for man a way to have a relationship with Him. In this God-man relationship, God is jealous of anything that threatens the love and trust which is the foundation of this relationship.

God refuses to allow us to share our loyalty to Him with other gods or spirit beings. He will not tolerate our division of allegiance between Him and other spirit beings. God is angered when man worships objects such as idols or images, as He states in the first of the Ten Commandments. All of these things can threaten the love and trust that God wants us to have in Him alone.

In a relationship between a husband and wife, jealousy would naturally result if one went outside of the relationship to have a need met which should be met inside the marriage relationship. For example, the wife might become jealous if the husband has his need for companionship met by another woman. Or the husband might become jealous if the wife has her financial needs met by someone else. Jealousy results when needs are met *outside* of the marriage relationship when they should be met *within*.

God is a jealous God. He does not want us to establish any relationship with people who are using the power of Satan. God is offended and jealous when man goes outside of his relationship with Him to have needs met that He Himself wants to meet. God intends that all of the needs which are met by the practitioners of the spirit world be met by Him through His body, the Church.

## GOD IS SOVEREIGN AND CANNOT BE MANIPULATED

All of the scriptural passages which tell of God's sovereignty (rule and authority) are beautifully summarized by King David in 1 Chronicles 29:11,12:

> Thine, O LORD, is the greatness and the power and the glory and the victory and the majesty, indeed everything that is in the heavens and the earth; Thine is the dominion, O LORD, and Thou dost exalt Thyself as head over all...and Thou dost rule over all...

God has absolute rule over His creation. In order for this to be true He must be all-knowing, all-powerful and all-present. If God had limitations in any of these areas, He could not be sovereign.

**God has sovereignty over nature.** Though God created the material universe to operate under certain principles or laws, these laws are subject to Him as their Creator. By this we mean that God can exercise His sovereignty over nature by suspending its laws for His purposes. These are called miracles because these are events which occur outside the natural laws. God showed His sovereignty over nature when He parted the Red Sea and the Jordan River, caused the walls of Jericho to fall, caused the sun to stand still, brought rain or drought at His will, healed the sick, and raised the dead. God created the laws of nature, but He is not bound by those laws.

**God has sovereignty over the spirit world.** The spirit world was created by Him. Though one-third of the spirit world (demons) is in rebellion against Him, these rebel spirits can exist for a short time only with God's permission. While God was on earth in the person of Jesus, He showed His authority over the spirit world by casting out many of these rebel spirits. The demonic spirit world never argued with the authority of God. It recognized His authority and submitted to it.

**God has sovereignty over man.** There seem to be two aspects of God's sovereign will as it relates to man. The first aspect of His will might be called His perfect will. The perfect will of God stands as God's unchangeable intentions and plans for man and the universe. In God's perfect will He chose for Himself a people and a nation, He came to earth to die on the cross, and He is going to return to earth to judge and redeem it. God also has a prescriptive will for man. God, as the Great Physician, has written prescriptions for man's spiritual health and well-being. These are His Ten Commandments, His teachings, and His example. God wrote these prescriptions for the good of man, so that man might enjoy a full and abundant relationship with God.

> When we speak of the decretive and the preceptive will of God, we use the word "will" in two different senses. By the former God has determined what He will do or what shall come to pass; in the latter He reveals to us what we are in duty bound to do. At the same time we should remember that the moral law, the rule of our life, is also in a sense the embodiment of the will of God. It is an expression of His holy nature and of what this naturally requires of all moral creatures (Berkhof 1941:79).

However, God's children all too often exercise their freedom and choose to disobey God's prescription. Though the prescription is unchangeable (Matthew 5:17,18), man's response is varied. But this failure on the part of man to obey God's prescriptive will does not hinder in any way God's perfect will.

This powerful and sovereign God of the universe cannot be manipulated by man; He will not be controlled for man's purposes or desires by such ways as magic. God cannot be manipulated because everything belongs to Him, including man, and because His plan for man has already been established. What can man offer God that He does not already have? What can man do for God that He can't do for Himself?

In times of calamity, marital problems, or serious sickness, people are forever making promises in exchange for God's resolution of the problem. But the important question remains: With what can man bribe God?

## Submission or control?

Dr. Paul Hiebert in "Discerning the Work of God" (1984a) shows the distinction between submission and control. The distinction is more of attitude than behavior. Because God is sovereign, He cannot to be controlled. Instead, those in a faith relationship with Him are required to submit to His will. Magic, on the other hand, is control of the spirits to bring about man's will.

Magic is the desire to control the spirit world for one's personal ends and purposes. For the shaman, this takes on the form of ritual or sacrifice in order to obligate the spirit mentor to perform as requested. But there is sometimes an element of magic in the Christianity of the Filipino.

One example of a magical "desire to control the spirit world," can be found in the misdirected prayers of many

Christians. Prayer is God-ordained communication with Him. There is an attitude of prayer, however, in which a person seeks to obligate God to do what is asked by praying at special hours or seasons, by praying for extended periods, or by prayer and fasting. These misdirected prayers reflect an attempt to control God, and fall into the category of magic. True prayer never seeks to control God. True prayer is communication with God which seeks to know God's will and submit oneself to Him.

Worship is a recognition of God's sovereignty and brings a desire on the part of the worshipper to subordinate himself to God. However, worship can degenerate to ritual that has control as its main purpose. Worship as submission, and not control, is the basis of Christianity. God desires that His people submit to Him in loving obedience, to do His will and achieve His goals. Subordination is easy when one realizes that submission is due to the Creator of the universe who loves man enough to send His only begotten Son to die for him.

From Scripture, it is apparent that God is sovereign in His rule of man and will not be manipulated to do man's bidding. God is jealous when His people use the power of the spirit world which can be manipulated by man. God intends to meet the needs of His people Himself. God will meet these needs within the context of a relationship which is characterized by submission to Him, and not in the context of manipulation or bribery.

## MEDIATORS BETWEEN GOD AND MAN

There is something quite comforting about a holy God in heaven. Though drawn to God, man is also terrified of His holiness. If God is living off in heaven, then maybe man can hide his life from God and somehow pass unnoticed. There may be some comfort in such thinking, for each person has a great deal to hide from God.

But such thinking, though comforting for the sinner, is not biblical because God is present everywhere. Since God is spirit, He is not subject to the limitations of space. The heavens and the earth are full of God (Jeremiah 23:24). "...He (God) is not far from each one of us; for in Him we live and move and exist..." (Acts 17:27, 28). Man is always and everywhere surrounded by the presence of God.

But the nearness of God does not imply that He is easy to approach. How can sinful man approach the holy Creator of the universe, who is the King of Kings and the Lord of Lords? Man does not want to approach God directly; he wants someone to go to Him on his behalf. Man has always wanted a mediator.

In Old Testament times, before Christ came to earth, the people of God were given a system of temple rituals or sacrifices which were offered by priests so that they would not have to approach God directly. The sins of the people were dealt with through the sacrificing of animals by the priests. Once a year, on the Day of Atonement, the high priest went into the Most Holy Place of the temple right into the presence of God. But before the high priest could enter the presence of God, he had to bring the blood of an animal sacrificed for his sin and the sin of the people. It was through this sacrificial blood that the high priest was cleansed of sin so that the holiness of God cannot destroy him. Once in God's presence, he also offered the sacrificial blood for the sins of the people. The high priest was the mediator between God and man.

Filipinos still feel the need for a mediator between them and God. Folk Catholicism has a whole system of intermediaries so that man does not have to approach God directly. There is, first of all the Virgin Mary. She is seen as the one who can best intercede on behalf of man, because she is the "mother of God." Then there are the saints who can be prayed to, with certain saints specializing in certain types of prayers. In the Philippines, the *Santo Niño* is one of the favorite objects of prayer. Here, one can pray directly to Jesus but he is in the approachable form of a child.

Finally, the priest acts as a mediator between God and man as he hears the confessions of the people. This system of mediators in Filipino folk Catholicism has some basis in the Old Testament Scriptures, which also spoke of the need for a mediator between God and man.

However, one single event in human history changed the need for mediators between God and man — the death of Jesus Christ on the cross. On His death, the curtain that separated the Most Holy Place from the rest of the temple was completely torn from the top to the bottom, laying open the Most Holy Place for the people of God to enter.

In order for the high priest to enter the presence of God he had to bring in sacrificial blood for his sin. For anyone to enter the presence of God today, the requirement is the same. A person must have sacrificial blood before he can enter the presence of the Holy God. However, the blood of animals will no longer suffice as the sacrificial blood because there has been a sacrifice far greater than that of an animal. Jesus died on the cross and shed His blood as the final sacrifice for man's sin.

> The blood of Jesus, His son, cleanses us from all sin.
> 1 John 1:7

The only thing separating God and man is sin. God sent His Son to die on the cross as a sacrifice by which man's sin can be washed away. But even though Christ has already died on the cross, not just anyone can go into the presence of God. Only those who enter with the sacrificial blood of Jesus dare enter into God's presence. The sacrificial blood of Jesus is still available today by faith.

Jesus is man's only mediator before God.

# Filipino Spirit World

> For there is one God, and one mediator also between God and men, the man Christ Jesus.
>
> 1 Timothy 2:5

God will accept no one else. It is God's plan that Man should do all of his business with Him through His Son, Jesus Christ. And the only way that a person can relate to God directly is if he has his sins forgiven by faith, confession and repentance. Without the forgiveness of sin, man cannot enter into the presence of the Holy God without being destroyed. But we can approach the throne of the King of Kings with the confidence that He will welcome us if we accept the sacrificial blood of Jesus which cleanses us from sin. At His throne, He will hear and answer our prayers so "that we may receive mercy and may find help in time of need." We no longer need human mediators when we know Jesus as our Savior and Lord.

> Since then we have a great high priest who has passed through the heavens, Jesus the Son of God, let us hold fast our confession. For we do not have a high priest who cannot sympathize with our weakness, but one who has been tempted in all things as we are, yet without sin. Let us therefore draw near with confidence to the throne of grace, that we may receive mercy and may find grace to help in time of need.
>
> Hebrews 4:14–16

True believers in Jesus Christ and His shed blood have no need for human mediators of God's grace and mercy. The believer has direct access to God's "throne of grace." One should be suspicious of those who set themselves up as mediators of God's grace. They may be putting themselves in the position that only Jesus Christ is to occupy. Jesus expects the believer to trust Him as the only mediator. To do otherwise is a violation of the trust relationship.

# THE TEST OF TRUST

The essence of Christianity is a trust relationship between God and man based on faith. This trust relationship can be violated when a believer goes outside of his relationship with God. This results in God's jealousy. The trust relationship can also be violated if the believer attempts to control God rather than submit to Him. And the relationship can be violated by using a human mediator, and not the mediator which God sent, Jesus. Violation of this trust relationship is sin.

## PROBLEMS FOR THE FILIPINO CHRISTIAN

It should be clear by now that there are serious problems that confront the Filipino Christian regarding the spirit world. We have focused on the following problems:

1. Western influence has caused the Filipino church to ignore the existence of the spirit world.

2. The fear of confrontation with the western Christian worldview has resulted in the "conspiracy of silence" concerning the spirit world.

3. Satan and his spirit world army attack man through possession, influence and temptation with the end of keeping man away from a trust relationship with God.

4. Because churches in the Philippines have focused on ultimate concerns, the Filipino has been forced to go to *out-of-church* practitioners in matters of everyday concerns. When God's people go to practitioners of the spirit world, they are putting themselves in a position of trusting the spirit who provides the knowledge and power which the *out-of-church* practitioners use. These spirits may be demonic and may desire to lure the believer from his relationship with God through Christ.

Whereas this chapter has dealt with the individual believer in a trust relationship with God, it has been the intention of this book to discuss the spirit world within the larger context of our churches. It is within the context of the Church that the glory and power of God is more fully realized. For this reason the prescription for dealing with spirit world problems will be offered for the church as the body of believers in the Philippines.

The church in the Philippines must be challenged to face these problems and develop Filipino solutions. The answer to the problems of the spirit world will not be found in western theology which denies the very existence of such problems. Rather, the answer lies in Filipinizing the church with regard to the spirit world from the Bible, thus providing an alternative to consulting *out-of-church* practitioners.

# 10
# FILIPINIZING THE CHURCH

Folk Christianity is the predominant religion of the Filipino people. This interesting blend of *other worldly* and *this worldly* spirit beliefs exists in the form and style of folk Catholicism and folk Protestantism.

## FOLK CHRISTIANITY AND THE FILIPINO CHURCH

It is important to make a distinction between folk Christianity and the church. Folk Christianity is the total religious system of the Filipino people. It includes the ultimate concerns of salvation, sin, forgiveness, heaven, hell, Christology, and other doctrines. But folk Christianity, as was suggested previously, also includes a very elaborate system of spirit world beings and practitioners. These spirit beings are part of this world and interact with man in his everyday concerns. The combination of the ultimate concerns and the everyday concerns is a merging of the *other worldly* spirit beings and the *this worldly* spirit beings. This combination is folk Christianity.

The organized church is generally a reflection of a Christian belief system. It emerges out of, and is formed by the belief system of Christian people. This is not the case in the Philippines. The Filipino church reflects only part of the belief system known as folk Christianity. So Filipino folk Christianity is a system of beliefs and practices that is part *in-church* and part *out-of-church*.

The split nature of folk Christianity is best understood in light of the fact that the church was brought to this country by westerners: first by the Spaniards and later by the Americans. When the institution of the church came to this country it was western in its theology and in its organization. It was even western in its architecture. Western church leaders judged harshly any theologizing that was not western in its approach and content. The result was that there was very little theologizing from an Asian or Filipino worldview and context (see chapter 1).

Dr. Rodrigo D. Tano, former president of Alliance Biblical Seminary, in his book *Theology in the Philippine Setting*, recognizes this situation when he says that,

> Christians in the Third World have long been passive and uncritical recipients of ready-made theological systems transmitted from the West. Consciously or unconsciously, they have been led to believe that the only valid way of doing theology is that which conforms to the theological systems in North America and Europe. This regrettable situation has not enhanced the intellectual and spiritual maturity of the churches overseas (1981:1).

Dr. Tano's statement is only partially true. He is right regarding the matters of ultimate concerns. The theological systems, in matters of ultimate concerns, have been imported with very little adaptation to the Philippine context. However, Filipinos have not been "passive and uncritical" in matters regarding their beliefs in a *this worldly* spirit world that deals with man in his everyday concerns. If Filipinos have indeed been passive regarding the existence and pertinence of the spirit world, these beliefs would have died out centuries ago. But because Filipinos were not passive, they have been able to withstand centuries of pressure from the western church which denies the spirit world's existence.

Filipinos have developed what Leonardo Mercado calls a "*barrio* theology."

> The word "*barrio*" here is not taken in the sense of rural only. It is taken in the encompassing reality that the majority of Filipinos have a Malayo-Polynesian heritage and are influenced much by animism. Most of the barrios exist in agricultural settings which certainly affect their lifestyle as well as way of thinking. Many of the Philippine cities have enclaves of rural society. People who go in and out of the city to the country know their traditional roots. *Barrio* theology then also applies to the city in the meaning of *barrio* as explained above (1979:49).

Now the difference between folk Christianity and the Filipino church can be seen. Folk Christianity is a total belief system which deals with the ultimate concerns of the *other worldly* God as well as the everyday concerns of the *this worldly* spirit world. The church in the Philippines, both Catholic and Protestant, does not reflect this total belief system. The church, because of its western origins and influence, is primarily involved with ultimate concerns. Since it is more of a reflection of the western worldview, it does not incorporate a belief in a *this worldly* spirit world.

## FILIPINIZING THE CHURCH: TEXT AND CONTEXT INTERACTION

Since the church in the Philippines, as an institution, largely ignores the existence of a *this worldly* spirit world, its continued belief is left to traditions and legends. This chapter aims to show that the church is the proper place to deal with the existence of the spirit world. The challenge is one of broadening the scope of the Church to include the spirit world and the Christian's relationship to it.

This challenge is the task of Filipinizing the church. The term "Filipinize the church" will be very uncomfortable to some, especially westerners, because it may suggest that culture is the determining factor in the theology and organization of the church. This is not the way the term is used here. The Filipinization of the church must have the Bible as its foundation in forming its theology and organization. But it also recognizes that theologizing is simply studying God as He makes Himself known in the culture of the Bible. For that theology to be useful, it must then be applied to the culture of the people to whom it is being taught. This process of Filipinizing the church is known today as contextualizing theology.

Dr. Tano accurately describes this process as an interaction between the text (Scripture) and the context (the Philippines). It is necessary for Filipino church leaders and thinkers to go directly to the source of theology — the Bible, to try to understand it and apply it in light of the real-life situation of the Filipino. Filipino theology must be done by those who know the real-life situation of the common *tao* (people). This should be done accurately and properly by Filipinos.

This interaction between the text and the context should affect both the church and the Filipino's folk Christianity. Presently, the belief system of the *this worldly* spirit world is outside the domain of the church. Bringing the Bible more fully to bear on the church will broaden its scope to incorporate a belief in the spirit world. This will happen because the Bible teaches a great deal about the spirit world.

The text–context interaction will also greatly affect folk Christianity. With a church that incorporates a belief in the spirit world, the Filipino will no longer feel the need to go outside the church to deal with his spirit world needs. This should gradually diminish the significance of folk Christianity as the church reflects the total belief system of the Filipino.

This Filipinizing of the church to include a theology of the spirit world will get little help from western theology, which gives only "lip service" to the existence of a *this worldly* spirit world. This is fortunate for the Filipinizing of the church. Without western theological sources, Filipino church leaders and thinkers will be forced to interact personally and directly with the text of Scripture and the context of the Philippines.

The Filipinization of the church, through the interaction of text and context, will also have its effects on the folk Christian belief system. The one aspect of folk Christianity that is Filipino is its animistic belief in the spirit world. This belief in a spirit world has existed in the framework of a "conspiracy of silence" with western church leaders. Consequently, the belief and use of the spirit world for everyday concerns is outside the realm of the church. This belief system is passed on from generation to generation within the family. It is based on traditions, legends, and practices which have been carried on for centuries. Filipinizing the church will bring the Bible to bear on these customs, traditions, and practices which should have its effects on folk Christianity. The result of bringing the Bible to bear on the spirit world belief system of folk Christianity may not be as dramatic as one may first think. As has been previously suggested, the spirit worldview of the Filipino regarding angels, Satan and demonization, is somewhat compatible with that of the Bible.

Presently there are aspects of Filipino folk Christianity which are *in-church* (ultimate concerns) and aspects which are *out-of-church* (the spirit world). It is the challenge of this book to show that some of what is *out-of-church* should be *in-church*. Therefore, the organized church should broaden its scope to include a biblical belief in a *this worldly* spirit world. The *out-of-church* spirit world needs to be biblically examined to determine which aspect should be brought into the domain of the church, which should remain *out-of-church* (secular), and which are wrong (sinful).

## SCIENCE, THE SPIRIT WORLD AND THE FILIPINO CHURCH

The Filipino Christian is increasingly facing the same challenge of science on his supernatural worldview which was experienced by the western church. However, this challenge is not coming to all parts of this culture at the same time because only a part of the society can avail itself of higher education, where this confrontation with science takes place. This leaves a society in which there is a great difference in groups in terms of education and, therefore, exposure to scientific knowledge and thinking.

These differences in educational levels produce wide variations in the blend between spirit world explanations and scientific explanations in the minds of Filipinos. Some Filipinos are at the scientific end of the scale, some are at the spirit world end of the scale and most are in the middle of the scale blending scientific and spirit world explanations.

The Filipino church must broaden its scope to be able to meet the Filipino people at any point on the scale between science and spirit world. For those Filipinos who are more toward the scientific end of the scale, there is already a western style theology which gives scientific explanations for anything that is *this worldly*. But for those Filipinos who have a strong belief in the *this worldly* spirit world, western theology has little or nothing to offer. Most Filipinos are at the spirit world end of the scale. Consequently the Filipino church, with its western theology, is not addressing itself to the spirit world belief of a large segment (possibly a majority) of the population. A large segment of the Filipino people are waiting for a message of good news which addresses itself to their beliefs and fears of the spirit world, and their immediate, everyday needs and concerns.

The animistic or spirit world beliefs of the Filipino have persisted because they are and have always been an *out-of-church* belief system. "Apparently the Filipino is still an animist at heart, in spite of four centuries of Roman Catholicism" (Bulatao 1980:148).

## Dr. Paul Hiebert's "Critical Contextualization"

In his syllabus for "Phenomenology and Institutions of Folk Religions" which he teaches at Fuller Theological Seminary, Dr. Paul Hiebert gives invaluable insight into dealing with traditional (folk) beliefs and rituals. He calls his approach to traditional beliefs and rituals, "critical contextualization" (Hiebert, 1984b:98).

### Rejection of all traditional beliefs

Dr. Hiebert examines the problem of outright rejection of all traditional beliefs. He shows that this leads to the Gospel appearing foreign and imported to both Christians and non-Christians within the culture. Outright rejection also leads to the problem of submersion, where traditional beliefs and rituals simply go underground away from the critical eyes of the missionaries and church leaders.

Rejection of all traditional beliefs and practices has been the main tactic of Protestant missions in the Philippines. Protestant missionaries ignored or condemned anything related to the Filipino spirit world. This resulted in submersion or the "conspiracy of silence" on this subject.

## Uncritical acceptance of traditional beliefs

However, Dr. Hiebert goes on to show that the uncritical acceptance of traditional beliefs and rituals leads to syncretism, the unacceptable mixture of animism and Christianity. Uncritical use of old beliefs and forms, in the end, leads to a mix in which the essence of the Gospel may be lost. Christianity then becomes a veneer covering the old religious ways (Hiebert, 1948b:98).

This uncritical acceptance has been the main tactic of Roman Catholic missions. Because of this, there are clearly animistic beliefs and practices within the Catholic Church. An example of such practice is the "blessing" of palm fronds which are then used to ward off evil spirits.

## Critical contextualization

Critical contextualization attempts to avoid the problems which are the result of outright rejection and uncritical acceptance. Its goal is "contextualization with preservation of the Gospel" (Hiebert 1984b:98).

There are three steps to critical contextualization. The first step involves open discussion of the traditional beliefs and practices of the people. This discussion must be without criticism or censure, or else the beliefs will simply be driven underground. Next, biblical instruction is given regarding those beliefs and practices which were brought up in the open discussion. Finally, a new belief and ritual system should be developed by
  (1) rejecting old beliefs and practices which are not biblical,
  (2) modifying the old beliefs and practices to make them compatible with Scripture, and
  (3) creating new beliefs and rituals which are compatible with Scripture, and also culturally appropriate.

It is the purpose of this book to stimulate this critical contextualization by providing a biblical basis for open discussion of the spirit world within the Filipino church. Critical contextualization means rejecting and modifying beliefs and rituals to make them scripturally and culturally appropriate. But there can be no critical contextualization unless the church begins teaching about the spirit world based on an interaction between the biblical text and the Filipino context. From that teaching, an alternative to *out-of-church* practitioners must emerge. Filipinos (like all people) will not reject old beliefs and rituals unless they are replaced with suitable alternatives. So, teaching and alternatives are the keys to the Filipinization of the church with respect to the spirit world.

# 11
# Teaching and Alternatives: Keys to Victory for the Church

God has given the believer power over the spirit world but God does not intend the believer to fight the spirit world alone. The Bible makes no mention of Christians who fought the battle of faith alone. God has called His people together into a body called the "church" so that they can encourage and equip each other to do battle against the evil spirit world of Satan.

The victory of the church in the Philippines against its fear of and dependence on the spirit world will require that the church broaden its scope of doctrine and practice to include the spirit world. This Filipinization of the church will require clear teaching on the spirit world and appropriate alternatives for members who are going to *out-of-church* practitioners of the spirit world.

The power for the church comes from the same source as the power for the individual believer: through the Holy Spirit. But this power is manifest or shown in the church through various gifts, ministries, and effects such as those listed in 1 Corinthians 12:4-11.

## The Struggle of the Church

The program of a church is often organized around this very central concept: When the church sees the human struggle to be against ignorance and superstition, it organizes schools to educate the people. When the church believes that a person's greatest struggle is political oppression, it may become politically active or even revolutionary. However, Scripture says,

> For our struggle is not against flesh and blood, but against the rulers, against the powers, against the world forces of this darkness, against the spiritual forces of wickedness in the heavenly places.
> Ephesians 6:12

For Paul, the focus of the church's struggle is not against flesh and blood. The struggle is not the personality conflicts between church members and leaders. It is not money or budgets for ministry and buildings. The real struggle is not a lack of trained leadership with planning and goal setting abilities. But often the church is misled into believing these as the real struggle. So what does the church do? It fights with the weapons of conflict management, budgeting, goal setting, planning, Bible schools, and seminaries. While all of these things are very good in themselves, they must never distract the church from its real struggle.

The struggle of the church is against Satan and his demons. This is what Paul is saying in Ephesians 6:12. These rulers, powers, and forces of darkness and wickedness are satanic and demonic, and they constitute the real struggle of the church. This evil spirit world causes many Filipinos to live in daily fear of offending a spirit which might cast a curse on them or their family. The only hope of victory against such an enemy is to fight with all the powers and gifts of the Holy Spirit.

## KNOWING THE ENEMY

In order to prepare for battle, it is essential to know the enemy and the place of battle. The Bible says that man's struggle is against Satan and his spiritual forces of wickedness in the heavenly places. The Filipino church must decide if this is indeed the main struggle. If man's primary struggle is against Satan and his forces, then the church must be organized for this primary battle.

There is little or no teaching about Satan and his demons and their relationship to man on this earth in the Filipino church. This is due to the influence, and in some cases, control of western Christians over the church in the Philippines.

In order for the Filipino church to prepare itself for the battle against the evil spirit world, it must stop ignoring the existence of a *this worldly* spirit world, provide clear teaching on the subject, and provide alternative responses to those needs now being met by *out-of-church* practitioners.

## Stop ignoring the existence of the spirit world

In one interview, I was told about the chairman of a Protestant church who would faithfully attend Wednesday night prayer meeting. After a prayer meeting one night, he was found in a graveyard saying incantations to the dead and following animistic rituals and formulas. On another occasion one evangelical pastor and a church leader consulted a *mananambal* after the medical doctor could not cure him.

These things happen because the church has continually ignored the spirit world belief system of Filipinos.

By ignoring the existence of a spirit world which has dealings with man, the church is ignoring a biblical fact: A *this worldly* spirit world is intimately and directly involved in the affairs of man.

## Provide clear teaching on the spirit world

The existence of a spirit world directly involved with man is biblical truth. As such, it should be preached from every pulpit and taught in every Christian education program. Clear biblical teaching about the spirit world and its relationship to man will move it out of the realm of superstition and into the realm of church doctrine. Biblical truth will remove the spirit world from the grip of legend and tradition, and put it into the hands of church doctrine.

This will mean that church leaders need to broaden the scope of their teaching to accommodate this Bible doctrine of the spirit world. This may bring judgment from the western Christian church which has largely ignored Bible teaching on this subject. But the preaching and teaching of the Bible on the subject of the spirit world will not bring judgment from God.

> Christo-paganism is, to a large extent, the result of unsound catechetical approaches. Nothing invites syncretism to develop more than letting the likes and dislikes of a new Christian community rather than sound theology decide the content and emphasis of the missionary message (Luzbetak 1970:248).

## SPIRITUAL NEEDS NOT YET MET BY THE CHURCH

Most Filipinos believe in a spirit world which is intimately involved in the affairs of man. They believe that some sickness is physical while other sickness can be caused by the spirit world. It is understood that most mental illnesses and emotional problems are psychological, while some are caused by spirits. The practitioners of the spirit world are believed to be able to handle sickness which is either physical or spirit-caused. The Bible supports most of these beliefs of the Filipino, while, for the most part, the church ignores them.

What alternatives does a person have when he believes that he has a sickness which is caused by a spirit? He would probably not go to a medical doctor for two reasons. First, he would not want to be ridiculed by the doctor for being superstitious. Second, he would probably believe that the doctor could not help him because the sickness was spiritual and not physical. Such a person would not go to the church leaders either for the same reasons. Besides fearing the ridicule of the church leaders, he would probably feel that his problem was outside the ability of the church, since nothing is ever mentioned on the subject. So the person is left with only one real alternative in dealing with what he believes to be a spirit-caused sickness: he must go to a practitioner of the spirit world or *mananambal*.

The church must provide an alternative for dealing with these spirit-caused needs of healing, spirit troubles, and divination. Unless an alternative is provided, the church leaves its members no choice except the *out-of-church* practitioners of the spirit world, who may be getting their power from Satan. Unless the church provides an alternative, its members will continue in their trust relationships with these spirit world practitioners.

> One of the main reasons for syncretic beliefs and practices is the fact that, as a rule, an innovation does not succeed in filling all the functions of the traditional counterpart (Luzbetak 1970:246).

## Teaching discernment of spirits

Jesus made distinctions between mental problems caused by a psychological imbalance and those problems caused by a spirit.

Though these distinctions seemed to be easy for Him to make, they are not as easy for the church.

For identifying which problems are psychological and what are spirit-caused, God has given another gift to His church. This is the gift of distinguishing spirits which is mentioned in 1 Corinthians 12:10. With this gift, the church needs to confront the spirit world only when the spirit world is the cause. This way the church does not begin seeing a demon "under every bush." Rather, the Holy Spirit gives to the person with this gift the ability to distinguish between psychological and spiritual problems.

The *out-of-church* practitioners have the power to discern when a person's problem is spirit world related, and when it is physical. They know that this is essential in determining the solution to the problem. This same power to distinguish spirit problems from physical and mental problems is essential for the church.

God has given the gift of discernment to His church, and He wants this gift to be exercised in the battle against the forces of the spirit world. When a demonic problem is identified through the gift of distinguishing or discerning spirits, then the church can deal directly with those demons. From the position of the church over Satan and with the power of the Holy Spirit, the demons or spirits can be commanded to depart from the troubled person "in the name of Jesus."

## The doctrine and practice of healing in the church

Most Christian churches in the Philippines believe, theologically, in divine healing. The Catholic Church has the Rite of Anointing which is used as a ritual for healing as well as for the "last rights." Evangelical Protestants have "prayer requests" in which the sick are prayed for.

In practice, however, most churches do not take healing seriously. They have "room" for divine healing as a doctrine, but as a practice it is minimized or ignored completely. It is mainly Pentecostals and Charismatics who give divine healing an important position in church practice. The Catholic Church rarely uses the Rite of Anointing in the context of divine healing. Protestants talk about divine healing, but in practice they generally pray for the sick with the same kind of expectations they have when praying for a new roof on the church.

Jesus took healing seriously. Everywhere He went, He healed the sick as part of His ministry and an extension of His message. Jesus healed in answer to a woman's faith (Matthew 9:20-22), and He healed even without faith on the part of the person (Luke 22:50-51). He healed in a variety of ways and means. It is difficult to find a specific pattern in Christ's healing, but it can be said without doubt that it was an important part of his ministry.

God has given the gift of healing to His Church so that His people do not have to go outside to practitioners of the spirit world. This gift of healing (1 Corinthians 12:9) is given to the Church for the common good of all the members. The gift is given by God so that His power can be displayed and released among His people.

The gift of distinguishing spirits is also important for recognizing what sicknesses have medical causes and what are caused by the spirit world. Satan has succeeded in creating much confusion in the Church over the gift of healing because Christians often fail to make this distinction. Some Christians have also begun to doubt God's power over the spirit world when they approached illnesses with medical causes as though they were caused by demons. Probably this is the reason most churches do not take healing seriously. As in the case of psychological problems, the Church needs to confront the spirit world only when the spirit world is the cause.

If the Church is going to help its people stop going to *out-of-church* spirit world practitioners, then it should get serious about the ministry of healing. Satan loves to attract the people of God away from Christ and the Church through his power, especially the power to heal. But God is jealous of this because He intends to meet this need in the context of the Church.

When the gift of healing is displayed in the church where the message of salvation by grace is preached, there is no doubt as to the source of power. The source of power for healing inside the church body is a gift from God. While the source of power for the spirit world practitioners outside the church is at least suspect and may be demonic.

Each church should take healing seriously. A theology of healing should be developed based on the Bible. But it is not enough to simply develop a theology. The church must also put it into practice among its members so that God can heal them.

The following is a good example of how one American missionary to the Philippines learned to look at divine healing in a new way:

> You know, we go to seminary for years to study the Bible so that we know what to believe and teach. But there are parts of the Bible which we read and then ignore. One day I was reading James 5:14–15 which reads, "Is anyone among you sick? Let him call for the elders of the churh, and let them pray over him, anointing him with oil in the name of the Lord; and the prayer offered in faith will restore one who is sick."

> I had read that text scores of times but had never taken divine healing very seriously. Sure, I had prayed for people who were sick, but I wasn't very serious about the outcome of my prayers. After reading this text I decided to take the Bible at its word. There was a member of the church in the hospital so I wanted to call the elders of the church and anoint him with oil. I didn't know what kind

of oil to use so I just brought along some cooking oil in a jar. I really didn't know what to do so I just poured oil on him. You know, God healed that person (Barnes:1983).

When the church really gets serious about healing, even its first faltering steps will be rewarded by the gift of healing which will unleash the power of God to His people. It is not wrong for Christians to go to medical doctors or hospitals when they are sick, but God is jealous when His people go to *out-of-church* spirit world practitioners for healing. He wants to meet that need Himself in the context of His relationship to His body, the Church.

## Confronting the spirit world directly

The Bible supports the Filipino belief that demons can cause people a great deal of mental as well as physical trouble. God intends His Church to exercise direct authority over these demons in the name of Jesus. All things are subject to the Church of which Christ is the head. Demons can be addressed directly, and commanded to depart, in the name of Jesus. God has provided the Church everything that it needs to confront the spirit world directly and be victorious.

It is not necessary to be a "specialist" to deal victoriously with the spirit world. God has granted to every believer position and power over Satan and his demons. For example, one woman cast a demon out of her house only a few hours after receiving Christ as her Savior.

Spirit world confrontation is not a new theology for the Church. But the practice of that aspect of theology will be very new to most. The Church will gain new insights into its position in the spirit world and its power over the spirit world as it exercises that position and power in confrontation and power encounter.

## Divination: Knowing the future or the One who holds the future

There seems to be such a great deal of uncertainty in the world today. So many of life's decisions are left to chance or fate. All of this uncertainty causes man a lot of anxiety and concern. For this reason, people go to diviners to learn about the future so that they have more information upon which to make better decisions. This information about the future reduces the unknown, lessening a person's anxiety about the future.

There are many areas of life in which the diviner can provide information from the spirit world. No doubt this supernatural information does reduce anxiety in the mind of the clients of these spirit world practitioners. But in order for it to be useful to the client, the client must have a great deal of faith and trust in the diviner. Without the faith and trust in the diviner, the client would not act on the information which was given.

The power to tell the future came to a slave-girl from a spirit of divination (Acts 16:16-18). This spirit was cast out by Paul like a demon. As with any practitioner of the spirit world, the power may be of Satan.

God has given to each individual and to the Church the gift of faith (1 Corinthians 12:9) to meet the need which the diviner provides. The diviner asks the client to put his faith in the information that he provides. God wants us to put our faith in Him.

Believers do not need to know the future if they know God, the One who holds the future. God wants us to put all of our confidence in Him and believe that He loves us and will take care of us. When a person really believes that God loves him and has the power to change the laws of the universe to meet his needs, then there is no need for anxiety.

> And we know that God causes all things to work together for good to those who love God, to those who are called according to His purpose.
>
> Romans 8:28

The believer has no need to know the future if he is living his life under the authority of the One who holds the future. God has concern for His people and the power to back up that concern. This should be a cause for peace and not anxiety. God would be jealous if His people did not trust His will for their future, but insisted on going outside of the God/man relationship to get information about the future. This would be an obvious sign that the person did not trust the One who holds the future.

## Prayer sharpens the church's focus on God

By giving His Holy Spirit, God has provided everything that the believer and the church needs to fight Satan. In the context of the church, God has provided gifts which are to be used for the good of His people. He has given all of these things through the Holy Spirit so that the believer need not go outside the church to have his spiritual needs met.

The gifts of the Spirit, the church's authority above all things that are Satanic, and the power of the Holy Spirit, are all to be exercised by the church. These doctrines are to be both taught and practiced. But in the exercise of His power, the believer and the church must never be distracted by the gift itself or the power. The victory over Satan and his demons is not in the church when the focus is upon the Source of Power. A distraction from God to His gifts and power will cause division and pride. But a focus on God, who gives gifts and power, will bring unity and victory to the church.

The best way for a church to maintain its proper focus on God in the midst of its battle against Satan is through prayer,

When the apostle Paul tells the believer and the church to "put on the full armor of God," (Ephesians 6:11) he follows that with the command to "pray at all times" (Ephesians 6:18). Prayer is the way in which spiritual weapons are used in the church's battle against Satan and his forces. Prayer reminds the believer that Christ is standing with him in this battle, and directs the believer's thoughts to God as the Source of power from which he is able to do battle.

Jesus devoted Himself to prayer while He walked on this earth. The early morning hours found Him on His knees before His heavenly Father. Jesus had His position as the Son of God, and His power from the Holy Spirit, but He still devoted Himself to prayer.

His disciples saw how devoted He was to prayer and asked Him if He would teach them how to pray. Jesus responded with an example and model of prayer known today as *The Lord's Prayer.* In the final sentence of that Prayer He gives three important points to remember:

1. "Thine is the kingdom. . ." The kingdom of heaven belongs exclusively to God, and He has set up Jesus as the King. To live in this kingdom, a person must be delivered by God's power out of the kingdom of Satan and be willing to do the will of King Jesus.

2. "Thine is the power. . ." The only power which can defeat Satan and his demons is the power of God Himself. But God has given this power to all who have cleansed themselves from sin and asked the Holy Spirit to possess them. He has also made His power available to the Church in the form of gifts and ministries.

3. "Thine is the glory. . ." God is only interested in glorifying Himself. His kingdom and His power are manifest on this earth so that He will be glorified. God desires that His people and His Church be a reflection of His glory.

## The danger of imbalance

*In-church* teaching and alternatives regarding the spirit world must be kept in balance with the other great doctrines of Scripture. Though the church must be engaged in spirit world conflict, the church is much more than that. If the spirit world is not placed in the context of all Christian doctrine and practices the church will become the place for "Christian magic" and be obsessed with the spirit world.

It must not be the goal of the church to simply replace traditional forms with Christian forms. We must seek change at the worldview level regarding man's relationship with God and let those changes spread throughout the rest of the culture. Though the Filipino and biblical spirit worldviews are similar, the Filipino Christian must see that God and His spirit world cannot be manipulated. God requires submission and will not be controlled.

## THE FINAL CHALLENGE

Filipinos believe in the existence of a *this worldly* spirit world and they are going to *out-of-church* practitioners who share their belief. The Bible supports the existence of the spirit world believed in by most Filipinos, with some modifications. The time is ripe and ready for the Filipinization of the church. The Bible must be brought to bear on the *out-of-church* practices and beliefs of the Filipino. The Bible must also be allowed to broaden the scope of the doctrine and practice of the church to include the *this worldly* spirit world of angels and demons.

When the church starts to believe that man's struggle is "not against flesh and blood" but against Satan and his "forces of wickedness in the heavenly places," then it will equip its people to do battle against such a foe. The struggle against Satan cannot be fought with ordinary weapons. The battle must be fought both individually and as a church with God's strength and weapons. Nothing less will give victory.

> "For the weapons of our warfare are not of the flesh, but divinely powerful."
> 2 Corinthians 10:4a

Filipino church leaders must decide on the focus of man's struggle and prepare their members. If Satan and his demons are man's primary struggle, then they must take on these divine weapons of warfare and teach their people to do the same.

It is the responsibility of the church to clearly teach the people about the believer's power against Satan and his demons, about the protection of angels, and the dangers of *out-of-church* spirit world practitioners.

The church in the Philippines must decide if it is going to go the way of western Christianity and ignore the existence of a *this worldly* spirit world. The alternative is to stand on its own, with the support of the Bible, and proclaim the existence of a spirit world and the believer's power against it.

God has given the church the good news that "the Son of God came for this purpose, that He might destroy the works of the devil" (1 John 3:8). There are millions of Filipinos who live in daily fear of and dependence on the spirit world. They are waiting to hear this message of good news. Is the church willing to proclaim it?

# BIBLIOGRAPHY

Aberle, D.F.
1966 —"Religio-Magical Phenomena and Power,Prediction, and Control." *Southwest Journal of Anthropology.* 22:221-230, (Autumn).

Adler, Mortimer J.
1982 — *The Angels and Us.* New York: MacMillan Publishing Co.

Ahrens, Theodor
1977 — "Concepts of Power in a Melanesian and Biblical Perspective." *Missiology* 5:141-173.

Ames, E.S.
1934 — "Shamanism," *Encyclopedia of Religion and Ethics.* Edinburgh: T & T Clark.

Anderson, Gerald H.
1969 — *Studies in Philippine Church History.* Ithaca, New York: Cornell University Press.

Ang, Gertrudes R.
1979 -- "The *Bayanihan* Spirit: Dead or Alive?" *Philippine Quarterly of Culture and Sociology* 7 (1-2):91-93, (March-June).

Anima, Nid
1978 — *Witchcraft, Filipino Style.* Quezon City: Omar Publications.

Arens, R.
1957 — "The Rice Ritual in the East Visayan Island, Philippines." *Folklore Studies* 16, 268-290.

1957 — "Animism in Philippine Rice Ritual," *Eastern World* II (9):36-37.

# BIBLIOGRAPHY

Barnes, Bruce
1983 — Baptist General Conference missionary from 1978 to 1983 in Leyte. Interview.

Barnett, Milton
1966 — "*Hiya*, Shame, and Guilt: Preliminary Consideration of the Concepts as Analytical Tools for Philippine Social Science." *Philippine Sociological Review*, XIV: 276-282.

Barton, R.F.
1941 — *The Religion of the Ifugao*. Menasha, Wisconsin: American Anthropological Association.

Berkhof, Hendrik
1962 — *Christ and the Powers*. Scottsdale, Pa.: Herald Press

Berkhof, Louis
1941 — *Systematic Theology*. Grand Rapids: Wm. B. Eerdmans Publishing Co.

Berzonsky, M.D.
1974 — "Reflectivity, Internality, and Animistic Thinking," *Child Development*, 45:785-789.

Blair, E.H. and Robertson, J.A.
1903 - 1908 — *The Philippine Islands 1493-1898*, 56 volumes, Cleveland: Arthur H. Clark Company.

Blatt, Harold R.
1963 — *Christian Focus on the Philippines*. Valley Forge, Pa.: American Baptist Foreign Mission Society.

Blodgett, R.
1981 — "What, Me Superstitious?" *Eternity* 32:37-39.

Boal, Barbara M.
1966 — "The Church in the Kond Hills: An Encounter with Animism." *The Church as Christian Community*. V.E.W. Hayward (ed.), London: Lutterworth Press 221:343.

1972 — "Casting Out Seven Devils." *International Review of Mission*, 61:342-356.

Bulatao, Jaime C.
1966 — "Split-level Christianity." *Philippine Sociological Review*, XIII:2 (April).

1968 — "Case Study of a Quezon City Poltergeist." *Philippine Studies*, (January), 178-188.

Burden, J.J.
1973 — "Magic and Divination in the Old Testament and Their Relevance for the Church in Africa," *Missionalia* 1 (3):103-112.

Busia, K.A.
1959 — "Ancestor Worship." *Practical Anthropology*, (January - February), 23-28.

Callaway, Godfrey
1936 — "Witchcraft." *International Review of Missions*, (April) 216-226.

Calvin, John
1977 — *Institutes of the Christian Religion*. Edited by John T. McNeill. Philadelphia: The Westminster Press.

Colpe, C.
1977 — "Syncretism and Secularization: Complementary and Antithetical Trends in New Religious Movements?" *History of Religions*, 17:158-176 (November).

Constantino, Josefino D.
1966 — "The Filipino Mental Make-up and Science." *Philippine Sociological Review*, 14:12-28.

Crapanzano, Vincent
1977 — *Case Studies in Spirit Possession*. New York: Wiley Inter-Science Publication.

Cullan, Vincent G.
1968 — "The Spirit World of Bukidnon." *Asian Folklore Studies* 27, pt. 2, 17-25.

Davies, R.
1978 — "Few Kind Words for Superstition." *Newsweek* 92:23, (November 20).

De Ridder, Richard R.
1978 — "God and the Gods: Reviewing the Biblical Roots." *Missiology: An International Review* 6:11-28.

De Wet, Chris R.
1981 — *Signs and Wonders in Church Growth*. M.A. Thesis, Fuller Seminary, Pasadena.

Demetrio, Francisco
1968 — "Toward a Classificication of *Bisayan* Folk Beliefs and Customs." *Philippine Studies* 16 (October) 663-689.

1969 — "*The Engkanto* Belief: An Essay in Interpretation."
*Philippine Studies* 17, (July) 586-596.

1973 — "Philippine Shamanism and Southeast Asia Parallels."
*Asian Studies II* (2):128-154, (August).

Diaz, Jesus
1966 — "The Christianization of the Philippines in its Theological Perspective." *Philippiniana Sacra,* vol. 1:207-215.

Dollar, Harold
1980 — *A Cross-Cultural Theology of Healing.* D.Miss Dissertation, Fuller Seminar, Pasadena.

Drury, Nevill
1982 — *The Shaman and Magician.* Boston: Routledge and Kegan Paul.

Durkeim, Emile
1966 — *The Elementary Forms of the Religious Life.* New York: The Free Press.

Elkins, Richard
1964 — "The *Anito* Taboo: A Manobo Cultural Unit." *Practical Anthropology* 11, (July-August), 185-188.

Elwood, Douglas J.
1970 — "A Theological Approach to Some Traditional Filipino Beliefs About Man." *Southeast Asia Journal of Theology* 12:37-53.

1971 — *Christ in the Philippine Context.* Quezon City: New Day Publishers.

Flattery, Phyllis
1968 — *Aspects of Divination in the Northern Philippines.* Chicago University, Philippine Studies Program, Department of Anthropology.

Frake, Charles O.
1961 — "The Diagnosis of Disease Among the *Subanun* of Mindanao." *American Anthropologist* 63:113-132.

Friedricksen, A.
1931 — "The Conflict of Jesus with the Unclean Spirits." *Theology* XXII (129):125-132.

Fu, V. R. and Billingham, R.E.
1980 — "Internality/Externality and Animistic Thinking." *Psychological Reports*, 46:815-819. June, pt. 1.

Galleon, Warlita K.
1976 — "Medicine Men (*Tambalans*) in Maasin." *Philippine Quarterly Journal of Culture and Sociology* 4(2):80-92, (June).

Gangel, Kenneth O.
1973 — "Using Filipino Culture to Enhance Christian Education." *Evangelical Missions Quarterly* 9:223-229.

Garcia, Lillian C.
1976 — "Some Observations on the *Gaba* Phenomenon." *Philippine Quarterly Journal of Culture and Sociology* 4(1):31-36 (March).

Glasser, Arthur F.
1982 — *Biblical Theology of Mission.* Class Syllabus, Fuller Theological Seminary, Pasadena, California.

1983b — Anonymous Interview

Hiebert, Paul G.
1976 — *Cultural Anthropology*. Philadelphia: J.B. Lippincott Company.

1982 — "The Flaw of the Excluded Middle." *Missiology: An International Review*, vol. X, No. 1 (January).

1984a — "Discerning the Work of God." Manuscript form.

1984b — "Phenomenology and Institutions of Folk Religions." Class syllabus, Fuller Theological Seminary. Pasadena.

Hislop, Stephen K.
1971 — "Animism: A Survey of Religious Beliefs Native to the Philippines." *Asian Studies* 9, no. 2 (August), 144-156.

Hollnsteiner, Mary R.
1963 — "Social Control and Filipino Personality." *Philippine Sociological Review*, XI:184-188.

Jocano, F. Landa
1965 — "Conversion and the Patterning of Christian Experience in Malitbog." Central Panay, Philippines. *Philippine Sociological Review* 13, (April), 96-119.

1966 — "Filipino Folk Catholicism." *Philippine Educational Forum* 15 no. 3, (November), 41-60.

1966 — "Cultural Context of Folk Medicine: Some Philippine Cases." *Philippine Sociological Review*, (January), 40-48.

1967 — "Agricultural Rituals in a Philippine Barrio."
*Philippine Sociological Review* 15, (January-April),
48-56.

Keesing, Felix M.
1962 — *The Ethnology of Northern Luzon.* Stanford: Stanford
University California Press.

Kraft, Charles H.
1979 — *Christianity in Culture.* Maryknoll, New York: Orbis
Books.

Kroeber, A.L.
1928 — *Peoples of the Philippines.* New York: American Museum of
Natural History.

Ladd, George Eldon
1959 — *The Gospel of the Kingdom.* Grand Rapids: Wm. B. Eerdmans
Publishing Company.

1974 — *The Presence of the Future.* Grand Rapids: Wm. B. Eerdmans
Publishing Company.

Lane, William L.
1975 — *The Gospel According to Mark.* Grand Rapids: Wm. B.
Eerdmans Publishing Company.

Langton, Edward
1942 — *Good and Evil Spirits: A Study of the Jewish and Christian
Doctrine.* New York: The MacMillan Co.

Latourette, Kenneth Scott
1975 — *A History of Christianity.* New York: Harper and Row.

Leslie, Charles (ed.)
1960 — *Anthropology of Folk Religion.* New York: Vintage Books.

Lessa, William A., and Vogt, Z.
1965 — *Reader In Comparative Religion: An Anthropological Approach.* New York: Harper and Row.

Lieban, Richard W.
1977 — *Cebuano Sorcery: Malign Magic in the Philippines.* Berkeley: University of California Press.

Luzbetak, Louis J.
1970 — *The Church and Cultures.* Pasadena: William Carey Library.

Malay, Paula Carolina
1957 — "Some Tagalog Folkways." *Journal of East Asiatic Studies,* 6:77.

McEwen, R.D. and Aseltine, H.E.
1979 — "Prayer in Primitive Religion." *Religious Studies* 15:99-106.

McGregor, Pedro
1966 — *Jesus of the Spirits.* New York: Stein and Day.

Mercado, Leonardo N.
1975 — *Elements of Filipino Theology.* Tacloban City: Divine Word University Publications.

1977 — *Filipino Religious Psychology.* Tacloban City: Divine Word University Publications.

1979 — *Contextual Theology in the Philippines.* Philippiniana Sacra, vol. 14:36-58.

Mezer, Robert P.
1970 — *Dynamic Psychiatry.* New York: Springer Publishing Company, Inc.

Michaelsen, Johanna
1982 — *The Beautiful Side of Evil.* Eugene, Oregon: Harvest House Publishers.

Miller, Elmer S.
1973 — "The Christian Missionary: Agent of Secularization." *Missiology* 1:99-107.

Montgomery, John W.
1976 — *Demon Possession.* Minneapolis: Bethany House Publishers.

Narayan, R.K.
1964 — *Gods, Demons, and Others.* New York: Viking Press.

Ndegger, William F. and Corrine
1966 — *Tarong: An Ilocos Barrio in the Philippines.* New York: John Wiley and Sons, Inc.

Neil, Stephen
1982 — *A History of Christian Missions.* New York: Penguin Books.

Newman, Philip
1962 — "When Technology Fails: Magic and Religion in New Guinea." *Natural History,* (February 6).

Nida, Eugene A. and Smalley, W.A.
1959 — *Introducing Animism.* New York: Friendship Press.

1975 — *Customs and Cultures.* Pasadena: William Carey Library.

Nordyke, Quentin, H.
1972 — *Animistic Aymaras and Church Growth.* M.A. Thesis, Fuller Seminary, Pasadena.

Norton, Mary G.
1960 — *Demon Experiences in Many Lands.* Chicago: Moody Press.

Nuguid, Nati
1972 — "The *Aswang* and Other Creatures of Philippine Lower Mythology." *Philippine Quarterly* 4, no. 3 (September) 28-36

Nurge, Ethel
1966 — *Life in a Leyte Village.* Seattle: University of Washington Press.

Oesterreich, T.K.
1974 — *Possession: Demoniacal and Others.* Secaucus, New Jersey: Citadel Press.

Peel, J.D.Y.
1969 — "Understanding Alien Belief Systems." *British Journal of Sociology* 20:69-84.

Phelan, John Leddy
1959 — *The Hispanization of the Philippines.* Madison: University of Wisconsin Press.

Radcliffe-Brown, A.R.
1952 — *Structure and Function in Primitive Society.* Glencoe, Illinois: The Free Press.

Rahmann, Rudolf
1974 — "Magico-religions and Medicinal Stones: A Case Study in Ethnomedicine." *Philippine Quarterly of Culture and Society* 2, no.1-2, (March-June), 81-88.

Ramos, Maximo
1967 — *The Creatures of Midnight: The Faded Deities of Luzon, the Visayas, and Mindanao.* Quezon City: Island Publishers.

1968 — "Belief in Ghouls in Contemporary Philippine Society." *Western Folklore*, 28 (July), 184-190.

1968 — "How Folk Beliefs Serve Society's Ends." *Hemisphere*, 12, (July), 8-14.

1970 — "The Aswang Syncrasy in Filipino Society." *Quarterly Review*, 3, no. 1, (March) 20-26.

1975 — "Folk Beliefs and Modernization." *Solidarity*, 9, no. 8 (November-December), 29-34.

Raum, Otto F.
1935 — "Magic and a Christian Policy." *International Review of Missions* (July) 358-365.

Rich, John A.
1970 — "Religious Acculturation in the Philippines." *Practical Anthropology*, vol. 17: 196-209.

Richards, John
1974 — *But Deliver Us from Evil: An Introduction to the Demonic Dimension in Pastoral Care.* London: Darton, Longman, and Todd.

Schneider, David J.
1971 — *Some Theological Aspects of Roman Catholicism's Responses to Lowland Filipino Spirit World Beliefs.* St. Louis: Concordia Seminary.

1974 — "Colossians 1:15-16 and the Philippine Spirit World." *Southeast Asia Journal of Theology.*

Sherman, Harold
1967 — *Wonder Healers of the Philippines.* London: Psychic Press Ltd.

Sitoy, T. Valentine, Jr.
1968 - 1969 — "The Encounter Between Christianity and Bukidnon Animism." *Southeast Asia Journal of Theology,* 10 (213): 53-79.

Skivington, S. Robert
1970 — *Baptist Methods of Church Growth in the Philippines.* MA Thesis, Fuller Seminary, Pasadena.

Sodusta, Jesucita L.
1983 — *Jamoyawon Ritual: A Territorial Concept.* Quezon City: University of the Philippines Press.

Staples, Russel L.
1982 — "Western Medicine and the Primal World View." *International Bulletin of Missionary Research,* 6 (2):70-71.

Strom, D.
1982 — "Why Knowing Animism is Necessary to Reach Hindus." *Evangelical Missions Quarterly* 18:146-151 (July).

Strong, Augustus H.
1907 — *Systematic Theology.* Valley Forge, PA.: Judson Press.

Sweet, William Warren
1975 — *The Story of Religion in America.* Grand Rapids: Baker Book House.


Tano, Rodrigo D.
1981 — *Theology in the Philippine Setting.* Quezon City: New Day Publishers.

Tippet, Alan R. Ed.
1972 — "Possessing the Philosophy of Animism for Christ." *Crucial Issues in Mission Tomorrow.* Chicago: Moody Press D.A. McGowan (ed.), 125-143.

1975 — "The Evangelization of Animists." *Let the Earth Hear His Voice.* Minneapolis: World Wide Publications, J. D. Douglas (ed.).

Toliver, Ralph
1970 — "Syncretism: A Specter Among Philippine Protestants." *Practical Anthropology* 17 (5):210-219.

Tuggy, A. L., and Toliver R.
1972 — *Seeing the Church in the Philippines.* Manila: OMF Publishers.

Turner, Harold Walter
1981 — "Religious Movements in Primal Societies." *Mission Focus* 9 (3): 11-38.

Unger, Merril F.
1961 — *Unger's Bible Dictionary.* Chicago: Moody Press.

Vandenbogaert, Chr.
1972 — *The Church in the Philippines at a Turning Point of its History.* Katholike Universiteit te Leuwen.

Verbrugge, M.
1982 — "Animism in Science." *Journal of Christian Reconstruction*, 8:79-107 (Winter).

Wax, Rosalie and Murray
1961 — "The Magical World View." *Journal for the Scientific Study of Religion*, 1:179-188.

Yates, R.
1980 — "Powers of Evil in the New Testament." *Evangelical Quarterly*, 52:97-111, (April)

# Index

Aaron *124*
"accommodation" *119-121*
afterlife *13, 17, 53*
Aglipayan *23*
Agpaoa, Tony *136-137*
*agta* *32*
All Souls' Day *21*
alternatives to out-of-church
    practices *156-157*
    teaching and *158-171*
American Christianity *29*
amulet *16, 21*
ancestral spirits *15-16*
"Angelic Spirit World" *56-73*
angels, angelology *27, 30, 57*
    fallen *75, 86-88, 95*
    messengers *67-69*
    ministry to God *65-66*
    ministry to man *66-67*
    nature of *59-61*
    number and organization
        *60-61*
    protectors *70-72*
    spectators *72-73*
animism *8, 13-18, 21, 23, 24, 43-45, 47*
    misconception about *8*
    strength of *8*
animist
    anecdote: animist and
        scientist *4-5*

animistic
    approach to "god" in sickness
        *35-40*
    religion *13*
    wake *9*
    worldview *8, 18-20, 26-48, 155*
*anito* *14-15*
*anting-anting* *16, 21*
Aquinas, Thomas *28*
astrology *92*
*aswang* *16*
Ave Maria *18*

*babaylan* *15*
Babylon *90*
baptism *17-18, 19, 22*
*barangan* *37-38*
*barrio* theology *151*
*Bathala* *13*
*baylanes* *15*
Black Nazarene *21, 120*
*buyag* *39, 117*
*buyagan* *39*

*capri* *32*
*catalonan* *15*
Catholicism *8*
    folk *19, 23-25, 149, 151*

Roman, added to pre-Spanish religion of the Philippines *17-22*
Charismatics *117, 164*
cherub, cherubim *62-65*
   Satan as a cherub *76-85*
Christ *84, 88, 115, 135*
Christian *134, 158*
   definition *134*
   Filipino *147-148*
   message *55*
Christianity *134, 147*
   folk *12-25, 149-151*
Christo-paganism *161*
confronting the spirit world *108-112, 166, 168-171*
"conspiracy of silence" *20-21, 45-46, 119-120, 147, 153,155*
conversion *23, 25*
Cornelius *69*
Creator Man *52-55*
Creator Spirit *49-55*
critical contextualization *156-157*
crucifix *21*
crystal ball *40, 92*

*da-ut* *38-39, 121*
Devil *82-83, 86-87, 96, 115*
demons *86*
   casting out *95, 108-112*
   fallen angels *75, 86-88, 95-96*
   sickness *94-96*
   specialization in demonic spirit world *91-94*
   variety in demonic spirit world *89-91*
demonic
   influence *103, 113-114*
   oppression/subjection *112*
   temptation *114-115*
"Demonic Spirit World" *86-96*
"Demonization" *97-116*
   clinical picture *103-104*
   influence *103-104, 113-114*
   scientific perspective *100-101*
   spirit world perspective *98-99*
   symptoms, and discernment of causes *94-96, 101-105*
demon oppression *112*
demon possession
   case study *105-108*
   casting out demons *94-96, 108-112*
   symptoms *99-100*
"Discerning Supernatural Powers" *117-133*
discerning
   causes of demonization *94, 101-105*
   gift of discerning spirits *104-105*
   practitioners of God *121-122, 131-133*
   teaching discernment of spirits *162-163*
divination *14-15, 40-42, 47, 92-94, 137-138, 167-168*
diviners *40-42*
   testing *131-133*

doctors  35
dragon  88
*dwende*  30, 32-33

Elijah  70
Elisha  58, 70
epilepsy  95, 99-100
ephiphenomena  104
Evangelical  113
everyday concerns  20, 42, 96, 118, 121, 151
exorcism  108-109
Ezekiel  63

fallen angels  75, 86-88, 94-96
familiar spirit  91
"Filipino Christian Worldview"  30-32
Filipino Christian
   problems for  147-148
Filipino pre-Spanish religion  13-17
Filipinos
   questions Filipinos ask when sick  35-37
"Filipinizing the Church"  48, 149-157, 158
   "Text and Context Interaction"  151-154
*fiscales*  20
folk Catholicism  19, 22-25, 149, 151
   and intermediaries  144-145

"Folk Christianity"  12-25, 42, 149-151
folk medicine  36
folk practitioner  36
folk Protestantism  24-25
fortune-tellers  40, 94
fortune-telling  92, 132
frogs  90

*gaba*  14, 16
Gabriel, angel  68
Garden of Eden  74, 80
Gerasene man  89, 93, 105-108
goats, shaggy, hairy  89
god, gods
   high, supreme  13-14
   lesser spirit being  16-17
   lower gods  14
"God Among Spirits, The"  49-55
God  27, 31, 37, 55, 60
   armor  115-116
   Creator Spirit  49-55
   Creator Man  52-55
   His character  138-140
   His sovereignty  140-142
   His will  141-142

healing in the church  163-166
Hiebert, Dr. Paul  10, 142, 155-156
high priest  144
*hilo*  39
holy water  21
Holy Spirit  104, 110-111, 113, 123-124, 159, 163

Iglesia ni Kristo  23
in-church practitioners  42-43, 118
in-church leaders' reaction to out-of-church practitioners  117-119
"in the name of Jesus"  93, 108, 116, 126, 130, 163

Jesus  82, 83, 88, 93-95, 101-102, 103, 106, 107-108, 110-111, 113-114, 123-124, 128-129, 131, 133, 145-147, 164, 166, 169

*Kabunian*  13
*kaluwalhatian*  17
"Keys to Victory for the Church"  158-171
King of Tyre  75

*lana*  14, 38
*Laon*  13
legion of demons  89, 106
life after death  13, 17, 53
Lilith  90
lower gods  14
Lucifer  74-85, 86-87
luck  40, 92
lying spirit  50-53, 55

magic  123-125, 142

magical arts  43
*mananagan*  44
*mananambal*  37-39, 43-44, 118-119, 135-136, 160, 162
*manunut-ho*  39, 44
*manghihilot*  44
*mangkukulam*  37, 44
man's nature  51
Mary Magdalene  89
mass  9
mediators between God and man  143-147
   Jesus, the only mediator  145-147
mediums  91
mental illness  104
mentor spirit  44, 135
Michael, archangel  61
missionary, missionaries  6, 8, 10, 23-25, 71, 165

natural world  5-6
nature  17, 53, 140
nature of man  51
night monster  90
*novenas*  21

ogre  32-33
oil  92, 165-166
ouija board  92
out-of-church practitioner  43-45, 117-119, 134-138, 160, 162-164, 171

190

# INDEX

palm branches  *21, 24, 120, 156*
*panalangin*  *14, 16*
pastor  *10, 42, 45, 46, 58, 60*
Paul  *72, 92-94, 109, 115, 127, 130, 159, 167, 169*
Pentecostals  *117, 164*
Peter  *69-70, 113*
Philip  *69*
*Pit Señor*  *22*
poltergeist  *104*
power, source of  *127-133*
   "Discerning Supernatural Powers"  *117*
practitioners of the supernatural  *42-45*
   diviner  *40-42, 131-133*
   in-church  *42-43*
   medical  *35, 136-137*
   out-of-church  *43-45, 117-119, 134-138, 160, 162-164, 171*
   spirit world  *37, 43, 96*
prayer  *36, 116, 118, 142-143, 168-169*
pre-Spanish religion of the Filipino  *13*
priest  *42, 45, 120*
prophecy  *132-133*
prophet  *132*
   false  *132*
   test of a  *131-133*
   Old Testament  *132-133*
Protestantism  *22-23*
   folk  *24-25*
   in the Philippines  *22-25*
   science and  *28-30*

psychic  *91-92*
psychic healers  *136*
purgatory  *21*

quack doctor  *36, 44*

Rationalism  *56*
rejecting science  *40-42*
   traditional beliefs  *34-35*
religious beliefs  *8, 12-13*
Rite of Anointing  *163-164*
Roman Catholic Church  *19, 22, 45*
Roman Catholicism
   and animism  *19, 22*
   added to Filipino pre-Spanish religion  *17-18*
   burial rites  *9*
   elements  *18*
   folk Catholicism  *19, 23-25, 149-151*
   on Filipino traditions  *17*
   policy on statues  *120*

sacrifices  *14, 15, 142*
   Old Testament Law  *144-145*
   Jesus as sacrifice  *18, 54*
saints  *21*
salvation  *18, 42, 56, 69, 84, 94, 112, 115, 125, 130, 132-133, 165*
*Santo Niño*  *21-22, 120, 144*
Satan  *27, 50-55, 74-76, 86, 96, 110*
   beauty of  *77-78, 85*

domain of  78-79
goal regarding man  82-85
origins  74-76
pride and subsequent fall  77-78, 87-88,
struggle of the church against  159-160
work of  81-85
satyr  90
Sceva  108-109
schizophrenia  100-101
science  28
 and demonization  100-105
 and divination  40-42
 and the spirit world  34-42, 47
 spirit world and the Filipino church  154-155
 and western worldview  27-30
seraphim  62
shaman  44, 45, 142
*sigbin*  30
sickness  35-40, 135-137
 and demons  94-96
 and Filipinos  35-39
 and healing  163-166
Simon, the sorcerer  122-125
Siquijor  36
sorcerer  39
sorcery  37-39, 44, 47, 122
sovereignty of God  140-142
"Specialization: A Result of Worldview Conflict"  42-45
specialization in demonic spirit world of in-church practitioners  42-43

of out-of-church practitioners  43-45
spiritists  43
spirits
 ancestral  15-16
 environmental  14
spirit beings  14-17, 32-33, 49, 52, 57, 62
spirit mentor  44, 135
spirit world practitioners  37-40, 43-45, 96
spiritualism  28
spiritual warfare  115-116
"split level Christianity"  19
split nature of folk Christianity  150
statues  21, 120
submersion  155
superstition  8-9, 20, 45
syncretism  156, 162

taboo  14, 16
tarot card  40, 92
tea leaves  40, 92, 103
"Teaching and Alternatives"  158-171
teaching discernment of spirits  162-163
testing diviners  131-133
test of a prophet  131-133
"Test of Trust"  134-148
"Theological Foundations"  49-55
*tuba*  14
*tut-ho*  39

ultimate concerns  *18, 20, 23, 25, 28-29, 31, 42-43, 47, 55, 118, 121, 151*

Virgin Mary  *30-31, 44, 61, 68, 135*

wake  *9*
*wakwak*  *16, 33*
"Western and Filipino worldviews"  *26-48*
western Christian worldview  *26-30*
western theology  *29, 150, 154*
witch, witches  *16, 27, 33*
witchcraft  *28, 37*
witch doctor  *9*
worldview  *26-48*
   animistic  *9*
   confrontation  *33-34*
   definition  *26*
   Filipino Christian  *30-33*
   scientific  *28-30*
   Western Christian  *26-30*
worship  *143*

# ABOUT THE AUTHOR

**Rodney L. Henry** served in the Philippines doing pastoral leadership training with the Seventh Day Baptist Philippines Convention from 1975-1985. He has a Master of Divinity degree and a Master of Theology in Mission from the Fuller Theological Seminary and the Fuller School of World Mission. He is currently pastoring the Denver Seventh Day Baptist Church in Denver, Colorado, USA.